AI4 AUTHORS

BUILD YOUR PUBLISHING EMPIRE WHILE SAVING TIME AND MONEY WITH THE POWER OF AI

JAMIE CULICAN

MELLE MELKUMIAN

DRAGON REALM PRESS

Published by Dragon Realm Press

Cape May Court House, New Jersey, USA

www.dragonrealmpress.com

ISBN: 979-8-3866-2695-2

Printed in the USA

First Edition: March 21, 2023

CONTENTS

DISCLAIMER

We have used the behemoth AI technology, GPT-4, who we call Zane, to help us write this book. Zane is an advanced artificial intelligence language model that has been trained on a massive amount of text data, allowing it to generate human-like language and writing styles.

We leveraged Zane's power to assist us in various stages of the writing process, including brainstorming ideas, generating outlines, and providing creative inspiration. We also used Zane for editing and proofreading, as well as data analysis and insights.

In fact, we actually used Zane to come up with the entire idea of teaching the integration of AI into the process to authors, but that is a story for a different thread.

Throughout the book, you'll see examples of how we incorporated Zane into our writing process. We believe that using AI technology can greatly enhance the creativity and efficiency of the writing process, and we're excited to share our experiences and insights with you.

Even if you're not familiar with GPT-4, don't worry. We'll explain what it is and how it works in a way that's easy to understand. We hope that by sharing our use of this cutting-edge technology, we can inspire and empower writers to explore the many possibilities that AI has to offer in the world of writing and publishing.

PART I

INTRODUCTION

From Melle

Whether you are eight, fifty-eight, or one-hundred-and-eight, you've seen incredible changes in technology throughout your lifetime. It seems like every few years there's a new innovation that transforms the way we live and work. Forget cars, planes, and computers. Those are ancient history. In the last thirty years alone we have witnessed unique and major transformations in technology that have impacted our daily lives.

Let's start with the internet. I remember sitting in the Sydney Conference Center one afternoon listening to a talk being given by none other than Bill Gates. As an employee at the Sydney Opera House I'd been given a free ticket to hear him speak about this thing he called "The Information SuperHighway." I still cringe when I think about the garish Powerpoint of a highway he showed to emphasize his point. (Oh, wait, Powerpoint is still a part of the fabric of the corporate world...some things don't change quickly.) I remember the confusion I felt about this new thing that was coming. Already a marketer, I imagined it like colorful marketing brochures on a computer screen. Little did I imagine how over the past few decades, the internet would revolutionize the way we manage our lives, connect globally, and acquire our goods. Years later I used eBay to buy an Aston Martin on the other side of the country for my own little Thelma and Louise adventure. Thank you, Internet.

Just when we all started to get used to the internet, though, along came...not just the mobile phone... but smartphones, which can be used for everything from making calls to taking photos to accessing the internet. While I often think of my phone as my camera, it also provides me with all the tools I need, at my fingertips, to manage my business, my finances, and my optics.

The next transformation hit me hard. I completed my Master in Fine Arts in film, and made an expensive effort to shoot my thesis on actual film because, well, film was still cool. In order to save money we'd spent most of our time shooting our college projects on digital video. Do you remember those mini-dv-tapes we used to slot in video cameras? Not many people do. Now, I watch my eleven year old use her phone to film, edit, and share a short video in minutes that would have taken us a week to produce. However, no one can complain about Netflix and Spotify, digital-first providers of media, which many of us can't get enough of.

Then, of course, we come to the subject of this book and perhaps one of the most prevalent changes in technology is the development of artificial intelligence (AI). Today, AI is used in many applications such as image recognition, natural language processing, and self-driving cars. It's pervasive in the very fabric of our daily lives with voice assistants, personalized recommendations and email spam filters. AI is everywhere and it is only growing larger.

And now, we have GPT-4, a revolutionary tool that is already changing the face of publishing. With its ability to generate human-like text, it has the potential to completely transform the way we write and publish books.

As an indie author, I'm excited and consciously cautious about the possibilities that GPT-4 brings to the table. With this tool, I can run my publishing business with greater insight, faster execution, and more in depth and personalized support. I can also write whole novels with it. (Much more on this later.) And therein lies a fountain of questions. What does this mean for the future of publishing? Will it lead to a world where books are written entirely by machines, with no human input whatsoever? Or will it simply free up our time and resources, allowing us to focus on the parts of the writing process that truly require human creativity and insight?

Only time will tell, but one thing is for sure: the publishing industry is on the cusp of a major revolution. In two years, we may not even recognize it. It's exciting to think about the possibilities that lie ahead, and it's up to us to embrace this new technology and use it to our advantage. So, let's get ready for the future of publishing, and see where GPT-4 takes us…

AI the Global Revolution

AI is transforming the world as we know it. The growth in the AI industry is projected to reach $390.9 billion by 2025*, which is a testament to its potential. However, with any technological advancement comes concerns about ethics and bias. It's crucial to keep these concerns in mind as we move forward into an AI-powered future.

* Reference: Zion Market Research - Artificial Intelligence Market by Technology (Machine Learning, Natural Language Processing, Image Processing, and Speech Recognition), By Application (Automotive, Healthcare, BFSI, Retail, and Others) - Global Industry Perspective, Comprehensive Analysis, and Forecast, 2018-2025.

Despite these concerns, there's no denying the potential benefits of AI. It's being used in amazing ways such as detecting fraud, personalizing medicine, and predicting maintenance needs. As much as we could stand here and share that it's valuable "to continue to explore the limitless possibilities of AI while also being mindful of its impact on society" (which is something GPT-4 suggested we write) the reality in our opinion is much more like Thanos, or as our kids like to call him The Big Purple Grape, "inevitable."

Adoption rates for AI technologies are also on the rise across a wide range of industries. According to a survey by Gartner, 37% of organizations have now implemented AI in some form, up from just 10% in 2015. This growth has been fueled in part by significant investment and funding in the AI space, with venture capital funding for AI startups reaching $40.1 billion in 2020.

The potential of AI is not limited to a select few. There are now over 2,000 AI-related courses available on platforms like Coursera and edX. This provides an opportunity for anyone with a passion for AI to acquire the skills and knowledge necessary to be part of the AI revolution.

Why AI Matters to Authors

As an author, you are familiar with the endless possibilities that language can offer in your storytelling. The very fabric of the publishing industry relies on the ability of writers to convey emotions, ideas, and stories through language. But now there's AI-powered tools such as GPT-4 that can write complete (if not completely convincing) books.

And, yes, we understand why writers feel threatened.

But, before we get to that, let's take a moment to seriously, look at what is this thing? I mean, we all saw the movie, A.I., but it's not that...yet. Simply put, AI refers to the development of computer systems that can perform tasks that typically require human intelligence, such as speech recognition, decision-making, and language processing. These key capabilities give it the potential to significantly streamline and automate various aspects of the writing and publishing process, saving authors time and effort while also improving the quality of their work.

One of the most significant applications of AI in writing is the creative process. AI-powered tools such as GPT-4 and Jarvis can generate ideas, outlines, and even entire paragraphs based on specific prompts or keywords. This AI-powered brainstorming can help authors overcome writer's block and even push the boundaries of their creative expression. By feeding the AI with specific parameters or prompts, authors can generate ideas and inspiration they may never have considered on their own.

Moreover, AI-powered tools can assist with editing and proofreading. Tools such as Grammarly and Hemingway use AI algorithms to identify and suggest corrections for grammar, syntax, and spelling errors. This can help authors improve the readability and clarity of their work, making it more accessible and enjoyable for readers.

In addition, AI-powered tools can assist with data analysis and insights. Tools like Bookstat and Amazon KDP reports can help authors track and analyze book sales, reader behavior, and market trends, providing valuable insights to inform marketing and promotional strategies.

This AI-powered data analysis can give authors an edge in the highly competitive publishing industry.

Okay, that's great, but what about the ethical considerations? Why are people HATING IN ALL CAPS on each other all over Facebook over this thing?

Well, there are ethical considerations and potential risks associated with AI. There are concerns about the potential for AI-generated content to undermine the originality and authenticity of creative work, as well as the potential for AI algorithms to perpetuate biases and discrimination. This is where the philosophy behind AI comes into play.

What you will hear us say over and over again is this:

AI is a tool.

In our opinion and experience, AI is not a replacement for human creativity. From what we've seen, AI cannot replicate the nuances of human emotion and experience that form the core of creative writing. As an author, it's important to be confident in the knowledge that the human touch is the hallmark of great storytelling.

Furthermore, when using AI, it's important to remain hyper vigilant about potential biases and ethical considerations. Since AI algorithms are only as objective as the data they are trained on, the ideal is that the data used to train AI is diverse and inclusive. Today efforts are being made to encourage diversity and inclusivity in the development and use of AI, including initiatives to address bias and increase representation of underrepresented groups. Authors must also be aware of the potential impact of AI-generated content on copyright laws and the publishing industry.

AI is a powerful tool that can help authors enhance their writing and publishing career. It can streamline the creative process, improve the quality of writing, and provide valuable insights into book sales and reader behavior. However, our perspective is that AI is a tool, not a replacement for human creativity. By approaching AI with caution and using it responsibly, authors can leverage its power to enhance their work while maintaining the integrity and authenticity of their creative vision. From a publishing point of view authors who engage with AI enabled tools can save time by auto-generating non-essential text, save money by automating tasks they previously paid for and increase revenue by providing book promotion tools.

From a 1950's Think Tank to ChatGPT

In 1956, a group of researchers gathered at Dartmouth College to lay the groundwork for AI as a field of study. The Dartmouth Conference, as it came to be known, marked the birth of AI research, and many of the attendees went on to become leading figures in the field.

In the decades that followed, AI research progressed rapidly, and by the 1970s, researchers were experimenting with rule-based systems that could mimic human reasoning. However, progress stalled in the 1980s, as the limitations of these rule-based systems became apparent.

It was not until the 1990s that progress in AI research began to accelerate again, driven by breakthroughs in machine learning and neural networks. Machine learning is a subset of AI that focuses on developing algorithms that can learn from and make predictions based on data. Neural networks are a type of machine learning algorithm that are modeled after the structure and function of the human brain.

In the early 2000s, AI research reached new heights with the development of deep learning algorithms. Deep learning is a type of neural network that can learn and make predictions based on vast amounts of data. Deep learning algorithms are the foundation of many of the AI-powered applications we see today, including image and speech recognition.

One notable example of AI we will explore is the GPT-4 language model, which was developed by OpenAI and released in 2020. GPT-4, short for "Generative Pre-trained Transformer 3," is a language model that can generate human-like text based on a given prompt. It is trained on a massive amount of text data and uses deep learning algorithms to generate text that is indistinguishable from text written by humans. (Or, is it?)

GPT-4 has many potential applications in the field of writing and publishing from creative brainstorming to deep research. In addition, GPT-4 can be used to assist with editing and proofreading. It can identify and suggest corrections for grammar, syntax, and spelling errors, helping authors improve the readability and clarity of their work.

As you can see, the potential of AI in the field of writing and publishing is vast. As AI technology continues to evolve, it is likely that we will see even more innovative and exciting applications of AI in the years to come. The possibilities are endless, and the future of AI in writing and publishing is certainly something to look forward to.

Here are some interesting statistics about how AI is being used, thought about and approached in the publishing industry:

1. According to a survey by the International Publishers Association, 60% of publishers are currently using or exploring the use of AI in some capacity.
2. AI is being used to help publishers analyze data on reader preferences and behavior, allowing them to better understand what readers want and how to market to them.
3. AI is also being used to automate various aspects of the publishing process, such as editing and typesetting.
4. In a survey of publishers by the London Book Fair, 25% of respondents said they believed AI would be the most transformative technology for the publishing industry in the next 5 years.

5. AI is being used to analyze book manuscripts to identify themes, characters, and even predict which books will become bestsellers.
6. AI is also being used to create personalized reading recommendations for individual readers, based on their reading history and preferences.
7. AI is being used to help publishers identify and combat piracy, by tracking online sources of pirated content and issuing takedown notices.

These are just a few examples of how AI is being used in the publishing industry. As AI technology continues to evolve, it's likely that we'll see even more innovative applications of AI in the world of publishing.

ChatGPT: An AI Writing Assistant for Authors

This book was researched, brainstormed, written, crafted, built, developed, processed, and revisioned using ChatGPT (see the case study at the end of the book). You may have heard about ChatGPT recently in the news because it is everywhere and we've mentioned it a dozen times since the start of the book. It is trained on a large corpus of diverse texts to generate responses to prompts, making it an ideal writing assistant for authors. It's hard to get the full impact of ChatGPT simply from a book so we really encourage you to log in to the app and start playing with it. I have had the pleasure of watching numerous people's faces as they watch ChatGPT in action for the first time. It's mind blowing.

One of the key benefits of using ChatGPT is its versatility. It can be used to assist authors in a wide range of writing tasks, such as brainstorming, drafting, editing, and even generating content. For instance, authors can use ChatGPT to generate ideas for plot development, character development, or even world-building in their stories. It can also help authors to come up with compelling headlines or taglines for their books or articles.

Another benefit of ChatGPT is its ability to assist authors in generating content for their social media platforms. With its deep learning capabilities, ChatGPT can generate social media posts that are engaging and relevant to the target audience. Additionally, ChatGPT can help authors to craft compelling email newsletters or marketing copy that resonates with their audience.

ChatGPT can also be used as a tool for improving the quality of writing. With its advanced natural language processing (NLP) capabilities, ChatGPT can analyze an author's writing style and suggest improvements to grammar, syntax, and vocabulary. This can help authors to refine their writing and produce higher quality work.

Moreover, ChatGPT can be used as a tool for content curation. It can analyze large volumes of text data to identify trends and patterns that can inform an author's writing. For example, ChatGPT can analyze customer reviews to identify areas of improvement for an author's work, or analyze industry news to identify emerging trends that an author can capitalize on.

Overall, ChatGPT is a versatile and powerful AI writing assistant that can help authors in a variety of ways, from generating ideas to improving the quality of their writing. With its advanced NLP capabilities and deep learning algorithms, ChatGPT is an ideal tool for authors looking to enhance their writing process and produce high-quality content.

From Jamie

The New World for Authors:

The world of publishing has undergone significant changes in the past decade, thanks to the rapid advancement of technology. These changes have had a profound impact on authors, providing them with new tools, platforms, and opportunities to reach readers and build their careers in the digital age.

One of the most significant changes has been the rise of e-books and digital publishing. Authors can now self-publish their work online and reach a global audience without the need for a traditional publishing contract. This has opened up new opportunities for emerging authors and allowed established authors to reach readers directly, without the need for a middleman.

As an emerging author at this time, I noticed a significant change happening in the publishing world. Authors were no longer limited to traditional publishing options, but had the opportunity to self-publish their work. However, with this new option came a new set of responsibilities that authors had to manage on their own. Instead of just writing the book and handing it off to a publisher, we were now responsible for all aspects of the publishing process. This took away from our writing time, ultimately slowing down book production.

Fortunately, the rise of AI has given authors the ability to reclaim their time and get back to what they do best - writing. With AI-powered tools such as ChatGPT, authors can receive assistance with tasks and get back to what they love most about being and author-writing.

Social media has also become an essential part of an author's marketing strategy. Platforms like Twitter, Facebook, TikTok and Instagram provide a way to connect with readers, build a following, and promote their work online. Authors can engage with their fans, share behind-the-scenes insights, and build a community around their work.

Artificial intelligence has also become more accessible and sophisticated in recent years. Tools like ChatGPT can assist authors with writing, editing, research, and marketing. These tools can save authors time and effort, allowing them to focus on the creative aspects of their work.

Mobile devices have also had a significant impact on the publishing industry. The rise of smartphones and tablets has made it easier for readers to access digital content on the go, creating new opportunities for authors to reach readers wherever they are. Authors can also take advantage of mobile technology to engage with readers through apps and other mobile-friendly platforms.

Self-publishing platforms like Amazon's Kindle Direct Publishing and IngramSpark have also made it easier and more affordable for authors to self-publish their work and distribute it to a global audience. This has leveled the playing field for authors, allowing them to compete with traditional publishing houses and reach readers around the world.

Finally, the popularity of audio books has surged in recent years, providing authors with new opportunities to reach readers who prefer to listen to books rather than read them. This has opened up new markets and created new revenue streams for authors.

The changes in technology over the past 10 years have had a significant impact on authors. They have provided new tools, platforms, and opportunities to reach readers and build their careers in the digital age. As technology continues to evolve, it will be interesting to see how it shapes the future of publishing and how authors adapt to new challenges and opportunities.

How can ChatGPT be helpful to authors?

Writing is an inherently creative and complex process, requiring a significant amount of time, effort, and dedication to bring a story to life. However, in recent years, the rapid advancement of technology has provided authors with a range of new tools and resources to help them overcome some of the challenges associated with writing and succeed in the digital age.

One of the most exciting and promising tools available to authors today is ChatGPT, an AI-powered chatbot that can assist with a wide range of writing-related tasks. ChatGPT has the potential to help authors improve their writing, streamline their workflow, and build a successful career in the digital age.

One of the key ways ChatGPT can assist authors is by generating new ideas for their writing. Many authors struggle with writer's block or find it difficult to come up with fresh ideas for their work. ChatGPT can help overcome this challenge by suggesting new plot twists, character developments, or other elements of the story. This can help authors stay inspired and creative, and ultimately produce work that is more engaging and satisfying.

In addition to generating ideas, ChatGPT can also provide authors with feedback on their writing. This can be especially helpful for authors who are looking to improve their craft or who are seeking feedback on a new project. ChatGPT can identify areas for improvement and offer suggestions for how to strengthen the writing, whether it's in terms of language, style, or structure. This feedback can help authors refine their work and ensure that it resonates with readers.

ChatGPT can also assist authors with research, providing access to a wealth of knowledge and resources related to their topic. This can save authors time and effort that would otherwise be spent on manual research. ChatGPT can help identify relevant research studies, articles, and other sources related to the topic, and even verify the accuracy of information and sources. This can ensure that authors produce work that is credible and well-researched, which can ultimately build trust and credibility with readers.

Editing and proofreading can be time-consuming and tedious tasks, but ChatGPT can help with that too. ChatGPT can identify errors in grammar, punctuation, and syntax, and even suggest alternative phrasing or word choices that can make the writing more engaging and effective. This can save authors time and effort, allowing them to focus on other aspects of their work, such as storytelling and character development.

Marketing and audience engagement are also important aspects of an author's career, and ChatGPT can assist with these tasks as well. ChatGPT can help authors create social media posts, marketing copy, and other promotional materials that are persuasive and effective in generating interest and sales. ChatGPT can also help authors engage with their readers and fans, answering questions, providing feedback, and building relationships that can lead to a loyal following. This can help authors build their brand and connect with their audience in a more meaningful way.

ChatGPT has the potential to revolutionize the way authors work and achieve their goals. By providing assistance with idea generation, feedback, research, editing and proofreading, marketing and audience engagement, ChatGPT can help authors improve their writing, save time and effort, and build a successful career in the digital age. As technology continues to evolve, it will be interesting to see how ChatGPT and other AI-powered tools shape the future of writing and publishing.

Overall, AI can help authors streamline their operations, improve content quality, and deliver more engaging and personalized content to their readers. By embracing AI, authors can position themselves for success in an increasingly digital and data-driven industry.

CHAPTER 1
AI AND ETHICS

One of the biggest concerns with AI is the potential for bias in the algorithms that power it. If left unchecked, these biases can perpetuate existing inequalities and marginalize underrepresented groups. A real-life example of this occurred in 2018 when Amazon's AI recruitment tool was found to be biased against women. The tool was trained on resumes submitted to Amazon over a 10-year period, which were predominantly from men. As a result, the AI system learned to favor male candidates and penalize resumes that included terms such as "women's," even for neutral job titles like "sales manager." This highlights the importance of testing and monitoring AI algorithms to ensure they are fair and unbiased.

REFERENCE:

Dastin, J. (2018, October 10). Amazon scraps secret AI recruiting tool that showed bias against women. Reuters.

ANOTHER LEGAL CONCERN with AI is its potential impact on copyright laws and intellectual property. Because AI has the ability to generate new content, it raises questions about who owns the copyright for AI-generated work. There have already been legal disputes over ownership of AI-generated works, which highlight the need for clear guidelines and regulations around the use of AI-generated content.

In addition to legal considerations, there are also ethical implications to using AI in writing and publishing. For example, using AI to generate content can blur the lines between what is considered original creative work and what is machine-generated content. It can also raise questions about authenticity and transparency in the creative process. As authors, it is important to consider the potential impact of AI on our creative work and to use these tools responsibly.

Throughout this book, we will explore these legal and ethical considerations in detail, providing practical advice for using AI in a responsible and effective way. We will also share real-life examples of how AI is being used in the publishing industry today, and provide insights into the exciting possibilities that AI presents for authors in both writing and publishing. By approaching AI with a critical eye and a commitment to responsible use, we can harness the power of this technology to enhance our writing and publishing careers, while upholding the integrity of the creative process.

Ethical considerations when using AI in both writing and publishing

One of the most significant ethical considerations when using AI in writing and publishing is the potential for bias in the algorithms that power it. These biases can perpetuate existing inequalities and marginalize underrepresented groups. For example, if an AI tool is trained on a dataset that predominantly includes white male writers, it may not be able to generate content that is representative of diverse perspectives. This can result in content that is skewed towards one particular viewpoint, leaving out valuable and important voices.

To avoid bias in AI-generated content, it is important to diversify the datasets that are used to train these algorithms. By including a wide range of voices and perspectives in the training data, AI can be used to generate content that is more inclusive and representative of diverse viewpoints.

Another ethical consideration is the potential for plagiarism. AI tools are capable of generating large amounts of content quickly, which can make it difficult to determine whether the content is original or not. If an author uses AI-generated content without proper attribution, they risk committing plagiarism.

To avoid plagiarism, AI-generated content can be properly attributed and sources cited. The key, however, is for authors to use AI-generated content as a starting point and add their own unique perspective and voice to the content. This step is crucial for building a brand and developing a unique voice, which are crucial to standing out as both an author and a business.

For those concerned about transparency and authenticity there are also important ethical considerations when using AI in writing and publishing. There is the opportunity when creating content to be transparent about the use of AI and to clearly distinguish between human-generated content and content that is generated by AI. This can help to maintain the authenticity of the creative process and ensure that readers know what they are reading. The challenge with this, however, is that in most cases AI-generated content is used as a base and the edits to it are so integrated, it isn't possible to separate out which word was written by the human and which was written by GPT-4.

By diversifying datasets, avoiding plagiarism, maintaining transparency and authenticity, and being mindful of the potential impact of AI on the publishing industry and broader society, authors can use AI in a responsible and effective way. By doing so, we can harness the power of this technology to enhance our writing and publishing careers, while also upholding the integrity of the creative process.

Potential biases in AI algorithms and how to avoid them

One of the most significant ethical considerations when using AI in writing and publishing is the potential for biases in the algorithms that power it. These biases can result in content skewed towards one particular viewpoint, leaving out valuable and important voices.

AI algorithms are trained on large datasets of information to learn how to make predictions and decisions. However, if the dataset is not diverse enough or if it contains biases, those biases can be reflected in the algorithm's outputs.

For example, if an AI tool is trained on a dataset that predominantly includes white male writers, it may not be able to generate content that is representative of diverse perspectives. This can result in content that is skewed towards one particular viewpoint, leaving out valuable and important voices. Similarly, if an AI tool is trained on a dataset that contains gender or racial biases, those can be reflected in the output.

To avoid biases in AI-generated content, it is important to diversify the datasets that are used to train these algorithms. By including a wide range of voices and perspectives in the training data, AI can be used to generate content that is more inclusive and representative of diverse viewpoints.

Another way to avoid biases in AI-generated content is to use a process called adversarial training. In adversarial training, an algorithm is trained to identify and correct biases in the training data. This can help to ensure the algorithm is not perpetuating biases in its outputs.

In addition to diversifying datasets and using adversarial training, it is important to conduct regular audits of AI algorithms to identify and address biases. These audits can help to ensure the algorithms are not perpetuating biases and are producing content that is inclusive and representative of diverse viewpoints.

It is also important to be aware of the potential for biases in AI tools that are used for tasks such as editing and proofreading. These tools may be biased towards certain writing styles or grammar rules, which can result in edits or suggestions that are not appropriate for all types of writing. It's valuable to use these tools as a starting point and to review the suggestions and edits carefully to ensure they align with the author's voice and style.

In conclusion, potential biases in AI algorithms are a significant ethical consideration when using AI in writing and publishing. By diversifying datasets, using adversarial training, conducting regular audits, being aware of biases in editing and proofreading tools, and ensuring input data is diverse and inclusive, authors can use AI in a responsible and effective way. By doing so, we can harness the power of this technology to enhance our writing and publishing careers, while also ensuring our content is inclusive and representative of diverse viewpoints.

How to ensure AI-generated content aligns with your values and beliefs

One of the most important ethical considerations when using AI in writing and publishing is ensuring the content generated aligns with your values and beliefs. AI algorithms can generate content quickly and efficiently, but they are not capable of understanding the nuances of human values and beliefs.

One way to ensure AI-generated content aligns with your values and beliefs is to provide clear guidance to the AI algorithm. This can include providing guidelines for language and tone, outlining key themes or concepts, and providing feedback on initial outputs. By doing this, you can help to ensure the AI-generated content is consistent with your values.

Another way to ensure that AI-generated content is aligned is to use a human-in-the-loop approach. In this approach, a human is involved in the content generation process, providing oversight and guidance to the AI algorithm. This can help to ensure the content generated is aligned with your values and beliefs, while also taking advantage of the speed and efficiency of AI-generated content.

It is also important to carefully review and edit AI-generated content. While AI-generated content can be a useful starting point, it is important to review it carefully to ensure it accurately reflects your voice and perspective. This can include reviewing the language, tone, and overall message of the content.

In addition to these steps, it is important to be aware of the limitations of AI-generated content. While AI algorithms can generate content quickly and efficiently, they are not capable of understanding the nuances of human values and beliefs. As a result, it is important to use AI-generated content as a starting point and to review it carefully to ensure it accurately reflects your voice and perspective.

AI algorithms can reflect the biases and stereotypes present in the data they are trained on, resulting in content that is not inclusive or representative of diverse perspectives. To avoid this, it is important to ensure that the input data used to train the AI algorithm is diverse and inclusive, and to conduct regular audits to identify and address biases in the output.

At the end of the day, ensuring AI-generated content aligns with your values and beliefs is a crucial ethical consideration when using AI in writing and publishing. By providing clear guidance to the AI algorithm, using a human-in-the-loop approach, carefully reviewing and editing content, being aware of potential misuses, and understanding the limitations and biases of AI-generated content, authors can use AI in a responsible and effective way.

At this point you may be sensing a theme...use AI as a starting point but not for final output. Throughout this book you will find that point made again and again as we believe it is truly the solution to many of the concerns over AI. The minute you truly integrate with AI output and make it your own, then these discussions tend to go away.

How to balance the benefits of AI with the importance of maintaining authenticity and originality in writing and publishing

As AI continues to play an increasingly important role in writing and publishing, it is essential to balance the benefits of AI with the importance of maintaining authenticity and originality. While AI-generated content can be a useful tool for generating ideas, enhancing creativity, and improving efficiency, it can also pose a risk to the uniqueness and authenticity of an author's work. Here are some strategies for balancing the benefits of AI with the importance of maintaining authenticity and originality.

Use AI-generated content as a starting point. For example, an author could use an AI-powered tool to generate ideas or outlines, but then develop these ideas further using their own unique perspective and voice. By doing so, the author can take advantage of the speed and efficiency of AI-generated content while still maintaining the authenticity.

Use AI-generated content in a complementary way. For example, an author could use an AI-powered editing tool to improve the grammar and style of their writing, but still rely on their own voice and perspective to convey their message.

By doing so, the author can enhance the quality of their work without sacrificing the authenticity and originality that make it unique.

Be aware of the potential ethical considerations. For example, there may be concerns around ownership of AI-generated content or the impact of AI on the job market for writers and editors. By being aware of these considerations and taking steps to address them, authors can use AI in a responsible and effective way.

By using AI-generated content as a starting point, using AI in a complementary way, and being aware of potential ethical considerations, authors can create writing that is both innovative and authentic. By doing so, we can harness the power of AI to enhance our writing and publishing careers, while still maintaining the unique perspectives and voices that make our work special.

CHAPTER 2
AI AND COPYRIGHT

As AI becomes more advanced, it is creating new challenges for the publishing industry, particularly in regards to copyright. With AI-generated content becoming increasingly prevalent, it is important for authors to understand how copyright laws apply to this type of content and how to protect their own work from potential infringement.

In this chapter, we will provide an overview of how copyright laws apply to AI-generated content, best practices for protecting your work, and the potential impact of AI on copyright laws and the publishing industry.

AI-generated content includes everything from articles and blog posts to books and music. The technology is capable of producing content that is virtually indistinguishable from that created by humans, leading to questions about who owns the rights to this content and how it can be used.

One of the most significant challenges posed by AI-generated content is that it can potentially infringe upon the copyrights of existing works. For example, an AI algorithm could produce a piece of writing that is very similar to an existing work, leading to questions about whether the new content is a derivative work or an original creation.

In addition to the potential for infringement, there are also questions about who owns the copyright for AI-generated content. In some cases, the copyright may belong to the person who created the AI algorithm or the company that developed the technology. In other cases, it may be unclear who owns the copyright, leading to legal disputes and uncertainty about how the content can be used.

Despite these challenges, AI technology also has the potential to greatly benefit the publishing industry. It can be used to generate new ideas and insights, improve the quality of writing and editing, and enhance the marketing and distribution of content.

In the following sections, we will explore how copyright laws apply to AI-generated content, as well as best practices for protecting your own work and using AI in compliance with copyright laws. We will also examine the potential impact of AI on copyright laws and the publishing industry, and discuss the ethical considerations involved in using this technology.

Real-life story: In 2019, the Associated Press (AP) began using AI technology to generate news articles about corporate earnings reports. The system, called Wordsmith, was able to analyze the data from the earnings reports and generate a news article in just a few seconds. While the use of AI technology allowed the AP to produce news articles faster, there were concerns about the potential impact on journalists' jobs and the question of who owns the copyright of the AI-generated content.

Reference:

"AP's use of AI brings automation to corporate earnings reports," Associated Press, July 1, 2019. [Online]. Available: https://apnews.com/arti-cle/5e6a64a6f9c342f78f48a5a1d00b72e5. [Accessed: February 28, 2023].

Overview of how copyright laws apply to AI-generated content

As AI technology becomes more advanced, there are growing concerns about how it intersects with copyright laws. The issue is particularly relevant in the publishing industry, where AI-generated content is becoming more common.

Copyright laws protect original works of authorship, including literary, artistic, musical, and other creative works. The laws give the creators of these works exclusive rights to control how they are used, distributed, and reproduced. Copyright laws also protect against the creation of derivative works, which are works that are based on or substantially similar to an existing copyrighted work.

When it comes to AI-generated content, there are questions about whether it constitutes a derivative work or an original work. For example, if an AI algorithm produces a piece of writing that is very similar to an existing work, is it a derivative work? Or is it an original work created by the AI algorithm? The answer to this question has significant implications for copyright law.

One of the most important factors in determining whether AI-generated content is an original work or a derivative work is the level of human input involved in its creation. In general, if a human is involved in the creative process, the resulting work will be considered an original work. However, if the AI algorithm operates entirely independently of human input, the resulting work may be considered a derivative work.

In some cases, the copyright for AI-generated content may belong to the person who created the AI algorithm or the company that developed the technology. However, in other cases, it may be unclear who owns the copyright, leading to legal disputes and uncertainty about how the content can be used.

In real life...

One high-profile example of the intersection between copyright law and AI-generated content involved a series of portraits created by a French art collective called Obvious.

The collective used an AI algorithm to create a series of portraits based on existing photographs.

The resulting portraits were sold at auction, but the sale was met with controversy when it was revealed that the algorithm used to create the portraits was based on code that was freely available online. The controversy raised questions about whether the portraits were truly original works, or whether they were derivative works based on the existing photographs.

In the end, the auction went ahead and the portraits were sold, but the controversy highlighted the need for clear guidelines and regulations around AI-generated content and copyright law. As AI technology continues to advance and become more prevalent, it is likely that similar issues will arise in the future, making it important for authors and publishers to stay informed about the latest developments in this area.

Best practices for protecting your work from infringement by AI-generated content

Protecting your work from infringement by AI-generated content can be a challenging task, but there are some best practices you can follow to minimize the risk. One of the most effective ways to protect your work is to regularly search the internet for potential infringement.

Fortunately, there are several tools available to help you with this task. One of the most popular tools is Copyscape, which allows you to check if your content has been copied or plagiarized on the internet. This tool compares your content with millions of web pages and highlights any matches found. You can then review the matches and take appropriate action, such as sending a takedown notice or filing a DMCA complaint.

Another useful tool is Google Alerts, which can be set up to notify you when new content matching your search terms is published online. You can create an alert for your book title, author name, or any other relevant keywords. This way, you can quickly identify any potential infringement and take appropriate action.

In addition to these tools, it's also a good practice to include copyright notices and watermarks on your digital content. This can discourage others from using your work without permission, as it will be clear that it is protected by copyright.

Another way to protect your work is to register it with the Copyright Office. By doing so, you have a legal record of your ownership of the content, which can help you in case of any infringement. Additionally, you may be eligible for statutory damages and attorney fees if your work is infringed upon and you have a valid registration.

Overall, it's essential to stay vigilant and take proactive measures to protect your work from AI-generated infringement. By using the tools and best practices outlined above, you can significantly reduce the risk of your work being copied or used without permission.

As AI technology continues to advance, the risk of infringement by AI-generated content increases for authors. In order to protect their work, authors need to be aware of best practices for safeguarding their content from potential AI-generated infringement.

One of the best practices for protecting your work from AI-generated infringement is to regularly monitor and search for potential infringements. This can be done by using various copyright monitoring tools that scan the internet for any unauthorized use of your content. It's also important to be proactive and register your copyright with the relevant authorities, as this can provide additional legal protection in the event of infringement.

Another important step is to clearly label your work with appropriate copyright notices, which can deter potential infringers from using your content without permission. These notices should include your name, the copyright symbol, the date of creation, and a statement indicating that the content is protected by copyright law. It's also important to include contact information so that potential infringers can easily reach out for permission to use your content.

In addition, it's important to be aware of the potential risks of using AI tools in your own content creation process. Some AI algorithms may inadvertently incorporate content from other copyrighted sources, leading to potential infringement issues. To mitigate this risk, it's important to carefully vet any AI tools you use and ensure that they have been designed with copyright considerations in mind.

One real-world example of the importance of protecting your work from AI-generated infringement is the case of a photographer who discovered that his photos were being used without permission on a major e-commerce platform. The platform had been using an AI-powered image recognition system to automatically tag and categorize photos uploaded by users, but the system had mistakenly tagged the photographer's photos as belonging to another user. As a result, the photographer's copyrighted images were being used without his consent, and he had to take legal action to have them removed from the platform.

This example highlights the importance of being proactive in protecting your work from potential infringement, and the need to stay vigilant in monitoring for unauthorized use. By taking steps to protect your work, including registering your copyright, clearly labeling your content, and vetting any AI tools you use, you can help safeguard your intellectual property from the risks posed by AI-generated content.

How to use AI in compliance with copyright laws

Using AI in compliance with copyright laws can be a complex topic, but there are several best practices you can follow to ensure that you are using AI-generated content legally and ethically. In this section, we will explore how to use AI in compliance with copyright laws and provide a real-world example of a company using AI in a copyright-compliant manner.

One of the most critical aspects of using AI in compliance with copyright laws is to ensure that you have the legal right to use the data you are feeding into the algorithm. This means that you should only use data that you own or have obtained legal permission to use. For example, if you are using AI to generate content for your book, you should only use your own research or data that you have obtained from credible sources.

Another best practice is to ensure that the AI-generated content is sufficiently transformative to qualify as fair use under copyright law. Fair use is a legal doctrine that allows for the limited use of copyrighted material without permission from the copyright owner. To qualify for fair use, the use of copyrighted material must be for purposes such as criticism, commentary, news reporting, teaching, scholarship, or research.

A real-world example of a company using AI in compliance with copyright laws is Jukin Media. Jukin Media is a media company that acquires and licenses user-generated content, such as viral videos, for use by traditional media companies. To ensure that they are using the content in compliance with copyright laws, Jukin Media uses AI to scan the content for any copyrighted material that may need to be removed or licensed.

Jukin Media's AI technology can identify copyrighted music, logos, and other protected content in the videos, which allows them to ensure that they are not infringing on any copyright laws. If copyrighted content is found in a video, Jukin Media contacts the original copyright owner to obtain the necessary license to use the content.

In addition to these best practices, it's essential to keep up with the latest developments in copyright law as they relate to AI. As AI technology evolves, so do the legal implications surrounding its use. Staying informed about changes in copyright law and seeking legal advice when necessary can help ensure that you are using AI-generated content in a legally compliant manner.

Overall, using AI in compliance with copyright laws requires careful attention to detail and adherence to best practices. By following these guidelines and staying informed about the latest developments in copyright law, you can use AI-generated content legally and ethically in your writing and publishing career.

The potential impact of AI-generated content on copyright laws and the publishing industry

As the use of AI in the publishing industry continues to grow, there are potential impacts on copyright laws that must be considered. Here are five key ways in which AI-generated content may impact copyright laws and the publishing industry:

1. Ownership of AI-generated content: One of the major challenges with AI-generated content is determining ownership. If AI is used to create a work, who owns the copyright? This question is complicated by the fact that many AI algorithms are created using large datasets that may contain copyrighted material. In some cases, the copyright ownership may be shared between the creator of the algorithm and the owner of the dataset.

2. Fair use and transformative works: Fair use allows for limited use of copyrighted material without permission for purposes such as criticism, commentary, and news reporting. With the rise of AI-generated content, the question of what constitutes fair use becomes more complex. For example, if an AI algorithm is used to create a work that includes copyrighted material, is it still considered fair use if the material is transformed or repurposed by the algorithm?

3. Infringement detection: As AI becomes more sophisticated, it may become easier for individuals and organizations to infringe on copyrighted material. However, AI can also be used to detect and prevent infringement. There are a number of tools available, such as Google's Search by Image and Tineye, which allow

copyright holders to search the internet for unauthorized use of their content.

4. Licensing agreements: As AI-generated content becomes more common, licensing agreements may need to be updated to address the use of AI. For example, a licensing agreement may need to specify whether AI can be used to create derivative works based on the original content.

5. New forms of content: AI-generated content opens up the possibility of new forms of content that may not fit neatly into existing copyright laws. For example, if an AI algorithm creates a piece of music or a painting, how does copyright law apply? These questions will need to be addressed as AI-generated content becomes more prevalent.

One real-world example of the potential impact of AI-generated content on copyright laws is the case of the "monkey selfie." In 2011, a photographer named David Slater set up a camera in the Indonesian jungle to take pictures of macaque monkeys. One of the monkeys took Slater's camera and snapped a selfie. The image went viral, and Slater claimed copyright ownership of the photo. However, animal rights group PETA argued that the monkey should be considered the copyright owner since it took the photo. The case was eventually settled out of court, with Slater agreeing to donate a portion of the profits from the photo to organizations that protect the habitats of macaque monkeys.

As AI continues to evolve and become more prevalent in the publishing industry, it is important to consider the potential impacts on copyright laws and the industry as a whole. By understanding these potential impacts, authors and publishers can take steps to protect their rights and ensure that AI is used in compliance with copyright laws.

CHAPTER 3
AI AND INTELLECTUAL PROPERTY

I ntellectual property refers to any original creation of the mind, such as inventions, literary and artistic works, and symbols, names, and images used in commerce. The protection of intellectual property is essential in the world of publishing, where authors and publishers rely on their works to generate revenue and establish their brand.

The increasing use of AI in the creation and processing of intellectual property has raised several legal and ethical questions. While AI can generate new intellectual property and streamline the creation process, it also raises questions about ownership, attribution, and the role of human creativity.

This chapter will provide an overview of how AI can be used to generate new intellectual property, the legal and ethical considerations surrounding AI-generated intellectual property, and the potential impact of AI on the creation and ownership of intellectual property in the publishing industry.

The use of AI in the creation of intellectual property is not a new phenomenon. For decades, scientists and researchers have been using AI to assist them in the discovery and creation of new inventions and scientific discoveries. One example of AI being used to aid in scientific discovery is the use of machine learning algorithms to analyze large datasets in fields such as genomics, drug discovery, and material science. By processing vast amounts of complex data, AI can identify patterns and relationships that would be difficult or impossible for humans to detect, leading to insights and breakthroughs in these fields. However, in recent years, the use of AI has expanded beyond traditional scientific research to include the creation of literary and artistic works.

One of the most significant challenges when it comes to AI-generated intellectual property is determining who owns the rights to the work. In the traditional model of intellectual property creation, the author or creator is typically the owner of the work. However, with AI-generated works, determining ownership can be a complex process.

In some cases, the creator of the AI system that generated the work may claim ownership of the work, while in other cases, the user who provided the data input may claim ownership. Additionally, the use of AI to create derivative works raises questions about who owns the rights to the original work.

Another challenge is attribution. While AI can generate new works, it lacks the ability to understand and interpret cultural and historical context, making it difficult to determine if the work is original or derivative. Additionally, the lack of attribution can make it challenging to determine the true origin of the work, which can have legal and financial implications.

Despite these challenges, AI has the potential to revolutionize the world of publishing by streamlining the creation process and generating new, innovative works. However, it is essential to consider the legal and ethical implications of AI-generated intellectual property and to ensure that the rights of creators and owners are protected.

In the next sections, we will explore the legal and ethical considerations surrounding AI-generated intellectual property and the potential impact of AI on the creation and ownership of intellectual property in the publishing industry.

Overview of how AI can be used to generate new intellectual property

One of the most exciting applications of AI in the publishing industry is the generation of new intellectual property. AI can be used to generate a wide range of content, from simple text to more complex media such as images, videos, and even music.

Using AI for content creation can provide authors with a

range of benefits, including increased productivity, enhanced creativity, and the ability to explore new ideas and concepts. For example, a writer may use an AI-powered tool to generate a range of prompts or ideas for their next novel or article, providing inspiration and new directions for their writing.

However, the use of AI for content creation also raises important questions about ownership and copyright. Who owns the rights to the content generated by AI? Is it the author who used the AI tool, the AI algorithm itself, or the company that created the tool?

The significance of these questions was brought to the forefront through the sale of an AI-generated portrait at Christie's Auction House in 2018. The French art collective Obvious created the portrait, titled "Portrait of Edmond de Belamy," using an algorithm that had been trained on historical portraits. Despite being entirely unique and original, the portrait fetched an astounding $432,500 at the auction, sparking a heated debate about the role of AI in art and creativity. This sale has raised important questions about the very nature of art and the boundaries of human creativity.

Reference: BBC News. (2018, October 26). AI Art Sells for $432,000 but Are Computers Creative? Retrieved from https://www.bbc.com/news/technology-45939535

Despite these challenges, the use of AI for content creation continues to grow in popularity, with many authors and publishers embracing the technology as a way to enhance their work. To help get your creative juices flowing, here are 10 introductory prompts that can be used with AI-powered content creation tools:

1. Generate a list of potential titles for your next book.
2. Create a short story based on a specific theme or genre.
3. Generate a poem based on a specific structure or form.
4. Develop a character profile for a protagonist or antagonist in your story.
5. Generate a plot outline for your next screenplay or film.
6. Create a script for a short video or animation.
7. Generate a range of headlines for your next article or blog post.
8. Develop a concept for a new product or service.
9. Generate a range of potential taglines or slogans for your brand.
10. Create a unique piece of art or graphic design.

Using AI for content creation can be a powerful tool for authors and publishers, but it's important to keep in mind the legal and ethical considerations surrounding intellectual property rights. By staying informed and using AI tools responsibly, authors can unlock new levels of creativity and productivity while also protecting their rights and ensuring that their work is original and unique.

The legal and ethical considerations surrounding AI-generated intellectual property

The development of AI has led to the creation of new forms of intellectual property, and as such, it has given rise to a number of legal and ethical considerations. There are key considerations authors should be aware of when using AI to generate intellectual property.

Legal considerations:

1. Ownership of AI-generated IP. One of the key legal considerations surrounding AI-generated IP is the question of ownership. Generally, intellectual property is owned by the person or entity that created it. However, when AI is used to generate IP, the question of ownership becomes more complex. In some cases, it may be unclear whether the IP is owned by the author or the AI system that generated it.

2. Patentability of AI-generated IP. In order for intellectual property to be patentable, it must meet certain criteria, such as being novel and non-obvious. When AI is used to generate IP, the question of patentability can become

complicated, as it may be difficult to determine whether the IP is truly novel and non-obvious.

3. Copyright protection for AI-generated IP. Copyright protection is automatically granted to original works of authorship, including literary and artistic works. When AI is used to generate IP, the question of copyright protection can be complicated, as it may be difficult to determine who is the author of the work.

Ethical considerations:

1. Bias in AI-generated IP. One of the key ethical considerations surrounding AI-generated IP is the potential for bias in the algorithms used to generate the IP. If the AI system is trained on biased data, it may generate IP that perpetuates existing biases.

2. Authenticity of AI-generated IP. Another ethical consideration surrounding AI-generated IP is the question of authenticity. Some may argue that AI-generated IP is not truly original, as it was created by a machine rather than a human being.

3. Impact on human creativity. Finally, there is a concern that the use of AI to generate IP may diminish the role of human creativity in the creative process. Some may argue that the use of

AI in this way is a form of "cheating" and that it undermines the value of human creativity.

Real-life example:

In 2018, a group of researchers at the University of Surrey in the UK developed an AI system that could compose music in the style of Johann Sebastian Bach. The system was trained on a dataset of Bach's compositions and used deep learning algorithms to generate new pieces of music that were similar in style and structure.

The researchers applied for a patent on the AI system, arguing that it was a novel invention that could produce unique works of music. However, the application was initially rejected by the European Patent Office, which argued that the system was merely a tool for generating music and not an invention in itself.

The case highlights the challenges of patenting AI-generated intellectual property and the need for clear guidelines and regulations in this area. It also raises questions about who should own the rights to AI-generated works and how they should be compensated for their use.

Reference: "AI creates new Bach-like chorales in world first" (University of Surrey, 2018) https://www.surrey.ac.uk/news/ai-creates-new-bach-chorales

As AI continues to advance, it is likely that we will see more cases of AI-generated intellectual property and the need for legal and ethical frameworks to protect the rights of creators and ensure fair compensation for the use of their works.

The potential impact of AI on the creation and ownership of intellectual property in the publishing industry

As AI continues to advance and become more prevalent in the publishing industry, it is crucial to consider its potential impact on the creation and ownership of intellectual property. While AI has the potential to revolutionize the way content is generated and consumed, it also raises important legal and ethical questions.

One potential impact of AI on intellectual property in the publishing industry is the increased speed and efficiency of content creation. AI-powered tools can analyze vast amounts of data and generate content at a faster rate than human writers, potentially leading to a larger volume of content being produced. This could have implications for copyright laws, as more content being generated could mean an increased risk of infringement.

Another impact of AI on intellectual property is the potential for AI-generated content to be owned by the AI itself, rather than the human creators who programmed it. This raises questions about the definition of authorship and ownership, as well as the legal rights of AI systems. If an AI system generates content without direct human input, who owns the resulting intellectual property?

Additionally, the use of AI in the creation of content

could blur the lines between what is considered original and what is considered derivative. While AI can generate new content based on existing data, it is not capable of truly original thought or creativity. This raises questions about the legitimacy of AI-generated content and its potential impact on the quality and authenticity of content in the publishing industry.

Despite these potential challenges, AI also has the potential to improve the accuracy and quality of intellectual property in the publishing industry. AI-powered tools can be used to analyze data and detect plagiarism, ensuring that content is original and free from infringement. Additionally, AI can be used to generate content in a way that is more personalized and relevant to individual readers, potentially increasing engagement and improving the overall quality of content.

Real-life example:

In 2019, a team of researchers at Rutgers University used AI to generate a completely original patent for a food container. The algorithm analyzed existing patents and created a new design that was never before seen. The researchers filed the patent and it was granted by the US Patent and Trademark Office. This example highlights the potential for AI to create entirely new intellectual property that could revolutionize industries and challenge traditional notions of authorship and ownership.

Reference: Soltani, S., Cheng, X., Liu, Y., & Gajos, K. Z. (2019). A Machine Learning Approach

to Patent Novelty Detection. Proceedings of the 2019 CHI Conference on Human Factors in Computing Systems, 477. doi:10.1145/3290605.3300837

As AI BECOMES MORE ADVANCED, it may be able to create works that are indistinguishable from those created by humans. This raises questions about the value of human creativity and the role of AI in the creative process. If AI can create works that are just as good as those created by humans, what is the value of human creativity and originality?

There is also the issue of ownership. With AI-generated works, it may not be clear who owns the rights to the work, especially if the AI was trained on a dataset that includes works from multiple authors. In this case, it may be difficult to determine who should be credited as the owner of the work and who should receive royalties or compensation for its use.

Additionally, AI can be used to replicate existing works, which raises questions about copyright infringement and fair use. If an AI system is trained on a large dataset of copyrighted works and then creates a new work that is similar to one of those works, does that constitute copyright infringement? Similarly, if an AI system is used to create derivative works based on existing works, who owns the rights to those works?

Overall, the potential impact of AI on the creation and ownership of intellectual property in the publishing industry is significant. It raises important ethical and legal considerations that need to be addressed as AI continues to advance and become more integrated into the creative process.

CHAPTER 4
AI AND CREATIVITY

A I has already made a significant impact on various industries, and the creative industry is no exception. AI has the ability to generate new content, ideas, and even art, leading to a debate about whether machines can replace human creativity. This chapter will explore the role of AI in the creative process and the potential impact on the definition of creativity and what it means to be an author.

We will begin by examining the history of AI in the creative industry, including its use in music, art, and writing. We will delve into the benefits and limitations of AI in creative fields, including the ability to generate new ideas and content at a faster rate and the potential loss of human creativity and originality. We will also explore the ethical and philosophical considerations surrounding the use of AI in creative industries, including the potential consequences for human employment and the impact on the value of originality and authenticity.

Furthermore, the chapter will provide insights into AI-powered creative tools such as Artbreeder and DALL·E, which can generate new and unique visual concepts and ideas. We will discuss how authors can use these tools to inspire and enhance their writing, while also considering the potential limitations of relying too heavily on AI-generated content.

This chapter will provide authors with a comprehensive understanding of the role of AI in creativity and the potential impact on the industry. It will offer practical advice on how to incorporate AI into the creative process while still maintaining the integrity of human creativity and originality.

The role of AI in the creative process

The creative process is often seen as a distinctly human endeavor, reliant on our unique abilities to think, imagine, and create. However, the rise of AI has introduced a new player into the mix, leading to questions about the role of AI in the creative process.

One area where AI is having a significant impact is in the realm of generating creative content. AI-powered tools such as GPT-4 and DALL·E are capable of generating text and images that are often indistinguishable from those created by humans. This has led to the development of AI-generated art, music, and even literature.

While some may be skeptical about the ability of AI to create truly original and unique content, the reality is that AI is already producing work that is being celebrated and appreciated by audiences. An example of an artistic endeavor with AI is the work of British artist Mario Klingemann, who uses machine learning algorithms to create abstract pieces of art. One of his famous works, called "Memories of Passersby I," is a constantly evolving piece created through the use of deep learning algorithms. The artwork has been appreciated by audiences for its unique and mesmerizing visuals.

Reference: "Artificial intelligence and creativity: Can machines make art?" by Madeleine Akrich, The Conversation, May 7, 2019, https://theconver sation.com/artificial-intelligence-and-creativity-can-machines-make-art-116470.

HOWEVER, the role of AI in the creative process is not limited to simply generating content. AI is also being used to assist human creators in the creative process. For example, tools like Artbreeder and Copy.ai use AI to help users generate new ideas and explore different creative directions. These tools can be especially useful for overcoming creative blocks and generating fresh ideas that may not have been considered otherwise.

Additionally, AI is being used to analyze and interpret creative works, providing insights and feedback that can help improve the final product. For example, a startup called Amper Music has developed an AI-powered music composition tool that can analyze a user's input and generate a custom soundtrack to match. The tool also provides feedback on elements like tempo, tone, and mood, allowing users to fine-tune their compositions.

While the use of AI in the creative process offers many benefits, there are also concerns about the potential impact on human creativity. Some worry that relying too heavily on AI could lead to a homogenization of creative works, with everything looking and sounding the same. Others fear that AI-generated content could become so prevalent that human creativity is rendered obsolete.

Ultimately, the role of AI in the creative process is still being defined, and it will likely continue to evolve as the technology advances. However, one thing is clear: AI is already playing a significant role in generating and assisting with creative content, and it will likely play an increasingly important role in the future. As such, it's important for creatives to be aware of the capabilities and limitations of AI in order to make the most of its potential.

The potential impact of AI on the definition of creativity and what it means to be an author

The emergence of AI in the creative process has sparked an ongoing debate about what it means to be creative and what role technology should play in the creative process. As AI becomes more advanced and more widely used, it is important to consider how it might impact our understanding of creativity and what it means to be an author.

One potential impact of AI on the definition of creativity is the blurring of the line between human and machine-generated content. As AI-generated content becomes more sophisticated, it may become increasingly difficult to distinguish between content created by humans and that created by machines. This raises questions about the uniqueness and originality of creative works, which are traditionally seen as essential components of creative output.

In the past, creativity has often been associated with the human ability to generate unique, innovative, and emotionally impactful ideas. However, with the development of AI, it is becoming increasingly clear that machines are capable of generating creative works that rival or even surpass those of humans. This has led some to question whether AI-generated content can truly be considered creative, or whether it is simply a product of sophisticated algorithms.

Another potential impact of AI on creativity is the shift in focus from the process of creating to the process of curating. As AI algorithms become more advanced, they are able to sift through vast amounts of data and generate content that is tailored to the preferences and tastes of individual users. This has the potential to fundamentally alter the way that creative works are produced and consumed, as the focus shifts from the process of creating to the process of selecting and refining content.

Despite these concerns, many argue that AI has the potential to expand the boundaries of creativity and enable us to create works that were previously impossible. For example, AI-generated music has been praised for its ability to create unique sounds and compositions that would be difficult for humans to produce. Similarly, AI-generated visual art has been lauded for its ability to create stunning and innovative designs.

Real-world examples of AI in the creative process abound. For instance, the music industry has seen a significant increase in the use of AI for music composition and production. AI algorithms are capable of generating melodies, chord progressions, and even entire songs that can be used by human composers to create new works. In the visual arts, AI has been used to create paintings, drawings, and other forms of art. In some cases, AI-generated art has been sold at auctions for thousands of dollars, highlighting the growing importance of AI in the art world.

The potential impact of AI on the definition of creativity and what it means to be an author is a topic of ongoing debate. While there are concerns about the impact of AI on the creative process, there are also many potential benefits to using AI in creative endeavors. Ultimately, the role of AI in creativity will depend on how it is used and how we as a society choose to define creativity in the digital age.

The ethical and philosophical considerations surrounding AI and creativity

The use of AI in the creative process raises important ethical and philosophical questions that authors and publishers must consider. An ethical concern is the potential for AI to create content that is inappropriate, offensive, or harmful. For example, AI-generated content may perpetuate harmful stereotypes or promote hate speech, which could have serious consequences for both the author and the publisher. It is important for authors and publishers to consider the potential risks associated with AI-generated content and take steps to mitigate these risks.

The philosophical considerations surrounding AI and creativity are equally important. Many people argue that creativity is a uniquely human trait, and that machines can never truly replicate the creative process. They argue that creativity involves more than just generating content; it also involves the emotional and intellectual processes that go into creating something new and unique. In this view, AI-generated content may lack the depth and complexity of human-generated content, and may never be able to fully replace the role of the author in the creative process.

On the other hand, some argue that AI has the potential to enhance creativity by providing new tools and resources for authors to explore. AI-powered brainstorming and collaboration tools, for example, can help authors generate new ideas and overcome creative blocks, while AI-generated content can serve as a source of inspiration for human authors. In this view, AI is seen as a complement to human creativity, rather than a replacement for it.

Ultimately, the ethical and philosophical considerations surrounding AI and creativity are complex and multifaceted. Authors and publishers must carefully consider the potential risks and benefits of using AI in the creative process, and take steps to ensure that the content generated by AI is used in a responsible and ethical manner. By doing so, they can harness the power of AI to enhance their creativity and produce truly innovative works.

PART II
WRITING

In Part 1, we explored the legal and ethical considerations when it comes to AI and its impact on the publishing industry. We have reviewed the potential biases in AI algorithms, the importance of ensuring AI-generated content aligns with your values and beliefs, and the balance between the benefits of AI and maintaining authenticity and originality in writing and publishing.

Now that we have addressed these concerns, let's dive into the exciting ways that AI can enhance and support your writing endeavors. In Part 2, we will explore how AI can revolutionize the writing process in areas such as brainstorming, collaboration, creative inspiration, editing, and proofreading.

AI-powered tools have the potential to make the writing

process more efficient and effective, allowing authors to focus on the creative aspects of their work while minimizing repetitive tasks. AI can provide support for authors at every stage of the writing process, from generating ideas to polishing the final product.

In this section, we will provide an overview of AI-powered tools for brainstorming such as GPT-4, Jarvis, and Copy.ai. We will explore how AI can help authors generate ideas, outlines, and content, and how to overcome writer's block with AI-powered brainstorming. We will also discuss the role of human creativity in combination with AI in the brainstorming process.

Next, we will discuss AI-powered tools for collaboration, such as Google Docs and Slack. We will explore how AI can help authors collaborate with others in the writing process, providing real-life examples of how AI-enabled collaboration tools have been used in the publishing industry. We will also provide best practices for using AI tools for collaboration.

In the section on creative inspiration, we will introduce AI-powered tools for creative inspiration such as Artbreeder and DALL·E. We will discuss how AI can help authors find visual and conceptual ideas for their writing and how to use AI-generated images and concepts in a way that is unique and original. We will also explore the role of human creativity in combination with AI in the creative inspiration process.

In the editing and proofreading section, we will provide

an overview of AI-powered tools for editing and proofreading, such as Grammarly, Hemingway, and ProWritingAid. We will explore how AI can help authors improve the quality of their writing, providing real-life examples of how AI-powered editing tools have been used in the publishing industry. We will also provide best practices for using AI tools for editing and proofreading.

By the end of Part 2, we hope to provide authors with a comprehensive understanding of how AI can support them in their writing endeavors, from generating ideas to polishing the final product. With the support of AI-powered tools, authors can focus on what they do best: creating innovative and thought-provoking works that will captivate their readers.

Roadmap to writing with AI

The writing process involves several steps from brainstorming to editing, and AI-enabled tools can make each step easier and more efficient. Here's a roadmap to writing with AI:

1. Brainstorming: You can use AI tools like Ideaflip or Emotion AI to generate new ideas and get inspiration for your writing. These tools can help you identify patterns and themes and provide suggestions for topics that match your interests and preferences.

2. Research: AI-enabled tools like Grammarly, Copyscape, and Turnitin can help you gather information and

conduct research for your writing. These tools can detect plagiarism, grammar errors, and spelling mistakes in real-time and give you suggestions to improve your writing.

3. Structure: AI tools like Jotterpad or Scrivener provide a structured framework to keep your ideas organized and make the writing process more manageable. These tools can help with structuring your work, outlining your argument, and keeping track of your progress.

4. Writing: AI-powered writing tools like AI Writer or Copy.ai can help make the writing process smoother, and fast by offering smart suggestions, phrase recommendations and more. These tools can improve your writing speed, decrease writer's block, and provide additional ideas.

5. Editing: AI tools like Hemingway Editor or ProWritingAid can help you with the final step of the writing process. These tools can analyze your writing, identify stylistic issues and recommend corrections, making sure your work is flawless and professional.

Overall, AI tools can provide invaluable support throughout the writing process. Whether you're looking to generate new ideas, conduct research, structure your writing, or perfect your work, there are many AI-powered tools available to help make writing easier and more efficient.

CHAPTER 5

BRAINSTORMING

B rainstorming is a crucial part of the writing process. It is the foundation of creativity, helping authors generate ideas, themes, and plots for their writing projects. However, sometimes even the most talented authors can find themselves stuck in a rut, struggling to come up with fresh ideas. This is where AI-powered tools for brainstorming can be invaluable.

We will explore the potential of AI-powered brainstorming tools for authors. We will provide an overview of these tools, including GPT-4, Jarvis, and Copy.ai, and explain how they can help authors generate ideas, outlines, and content. We will also discuss how AI can help authors overcome writer's block and the role of human creativity in combination with AI in the brainstorming process.

In the following sections, we will provide a detailed overview of the most popular AI-powered brainstorming tools currently available. We will discuss the unique features and capabilities of each tool, provide real-life examples of how they have been used in the publishing industry, and offer best practices for using these tools effectively.

Overview of AI-powered tools for brainstorming such as GPT-4, Jarvis, and Copy.ai

In recent years, AI-powered tools have become an increasingly popular way for authors to enhance their brainstorming process. These tools can generate ideas, outlines, and even complete content, allowing authors to focus on the creative aspects of writing rather than getting bogged down in the details.

Some of the most popular AI-powered tools for brainstorming include GPT-4, Jarvis, and Copy.ai. These tools use machine learning algorithms to generate text based on prompts and examples provided by the user. This allows for quick and easy brainstorming sessions without the need for extensive research or planning.

GPT-4, for example, is a language prediction model developed by OpenAI. It can generate human-like responses to text prompts and has been used to create everything from news articles to poetry. Jarvis, on the other hand, is a personal AI assistant developed by Mark Zuckerberg that can help users with a variety of tasks, including generating content based on user prompts.

Copy.ai is another popular AI-powered tool for brainstorming, offering a variety of features including text generation, headline analysis, and more. It uses a combination of machine learning algorithms and natural language processing to analyze user input and generate high-quality content.

One of the major advantages of these AI-powered tools is their ability to quickly generate a large amount of content. This can be especially useful for authors who are struggling with writer's block or who need to generate ideas quickly for a deadline.

However, it is important for authors to be aware of the limitations of these tools and to use them according to their own ethics. While AI-generated content can be a useful tool for brainstorming and generating ideas, it should not be considered a substitute for original, creative content. It is also important to be aware of any potential biases in the algorithms used by the tools you are using and ensure the content generated aligns with the author's values and beliefs.

Overall, the use of AI-powered tools for brainstorming can be a valuable asset for authors looking to enhance their writing process. However, it is important for authors to use these tools responsibly and to balance the benefits of AI with the importance of maintaining authenticity and originality in writing.

Brainstorming Tools

Tool	Features	Rating
GPT-3	Generates human-like text based on prompts	⋆⋆⋆⋆
Jarvis	Generates outlines and ideas based on user input	⋆⋆⋆
Copy.ai	Generates marketing copy, slogans, and descriptions	⋆⋆⋆⋆
Ideaflip	Allows for visual brainstorming and collaboration	⋆⋆⋆
MindMup	Creates mind maps and diagrams for brainstorming	⋆⋆
Coggle	Creates mind maps and diagrams for brainstorming and collaboration	⋆⋆⋆
Milanote	Visual brainstorming and collaboration tool with various templates	⋆⋆⋆⋆

PLEASE NOTE that this is just an example and the features and ratings may vary depending on the research and analysis conducted.

How AI can help authors with generating ideas, outlines, and content

AI can be a powerful tool for authors who struggle with writer's block or finding inspiration. AI-powered tools for brainstorming, such as GPT-4, Jarvis, and Copy.ai, can also help generate ideas, outlines, and even content.

One way AI can assist in generating ideas is by analyzing existing content to identify trends and patterns. For example, GPT-4 can analyze text and generate new content based on patterns it identifies in the text. This can be a helpful tool for authors who are struggling to come up with new ideas.

AI can also assist in creating outlines for writing projects. Tools such as Jarvis can generate outlines based on keywords and phrases, allowing authors to quickly get a sense of the structure of their writing project. This can be particularly helpful for authors who are starting a new project or who are struggling to organize their thoughts.

In addition to generating ideas and outlines, AI can also be used to create content. For example, Copy.ai is a tool that uses AI to generate short-form content such as social media posts, product descriptions, and headlines. While this type of content may not be suitable for longer form writing projects, it can be a useful tool for authors who need to quickly generate content for marketing or promotional purposes.

Overall, AI-powered tools for brainstorming can be a valuable asset for authors looking to enhance their writing process. By generating ideas, outlines, and content, these tools can help authors overcome writer's block and find inspiration for their writing projects.

How to overcome writer's block with AI-powered brainstorming

Writer's block is a common phenomenon among authors that can often impede their creativity and progress in their writing projects. Fortunately, AI-powered brainstorming tools have emerged as a solution to this problem, providing writers with a new approach to overcome writer's block and generate fresh ideas.

AI-powered brainstorming tools like GPT-4, Jarvis, and Copy.ai can help authors overcome writer's block in various ways. First and foremost, these tools offer a vast database of knowledge that can serve as a starting point for writers to build on. They can also provide authors with unique prompts and suggestions that can spark creativity and encourage them to think outside of the box.

One of the most significant benefits of using AI-powered brainstorming tools to overcome writer's block is the ability to explore different angles and perspectives on a particular topic. These tools can help writers approach their work from various perspectives, enabling them to think creatively and generate fresh ideas that they may not have thought of otherwise.

AI-powered brainstorming tools can also assist writers in creating outlines for their work, breaking down larger ideas into more manageable components. This feature can be especially helpful for writers who struggle to structure their work cohesively or need guidance in creating a clear roadmap for their writing projects.

In addition, AI-powered brainstorming tools can assist authors in generating content. By providing suggestions for sentence structure, vocabulary, and tone, these tools can enhance the quality of the content and ensure that it aligns with the author's vision.

AI-powered brainstorming tools provide authors with a new way to approach their writing projects and overcome writer's block. By providing unique prompts and suggestions, enabling writers to explore different angles, assisting with outlining and content creation, and enhancing the quality of the content, these tools can be a valuable asset to any author's writing process.

The role of human creativity in combination with AI in the brainstorming process

In the creative process, human creativity and AI can complement each other in powerful ways. While AI can generate vast amounts of data and provide suggestions for inspiration, humans can provide the critical thinking and emotional intelligence necessary to make the final decisions and inject their unique perspective into the work.

It is essential to remember that AI is not a replacement for human creativity, but rather a tool to enhance and support it. As an author, it is still your job to determine the direction of your work, make creative decisions, and inject your unique voice and perspective into your writing.

When using AI-powered brainstorming tools, it is important to approach them with a critical eye and use them as a starting point rather than a final solution. By combining the power of AI with human creativity, authors can overcome writer's block, generate new ideas, and create more original and innovative content.

Overall, the collaboration between human creativity and AI can lead to exciting new possibilities for authors in the brainstorming process. By utilizing the strengths of both, authors can achieve a level of creativity and innovation that was once impossible.

CHAPTER 6
COLLABORATION

Before we started working together in business, we collaborated together on a young adult steampunk dragon reverse harem series and, yes, that's a thing… For most authors collaboration at some point in the process is a crucial aspect of any successful writing project. It is an opportunity to bring together different perspectives, ideas, and skills to create a work that is greater than the sum of its parts. However, collaborating with others can also be challenging, as it requires effective communication, coordination, and a clear understanding of each person's role and contribution.

Fortunately, AI-powered collaboration tools are available to help streamline and enhance the collaborative writing process. From real-time communication and project management to content creation and editing, these tools can save time and improve efficiency while maintaining the quality of the work.

This chapter will explore the various AI-powered collaboration tools available to authors and provide insights into their benefits and limitations.

Topics covered in this chapter:

- The benefits of AI-powered collaboration tools
- Common AI-powered collaboration tools, including Google Docs, Slack, and Trello
- How AI can enhance the collaborative writing process, such as providing real-time feedback and suggesting edits
- Legal and ethical considerations when using AI-powered collaboration tools, such as data privacy and ownership
- Best practices for using AI-powered collaboration tools effectively, including clear communication and setting expectations.

Throughout this chapter, we will use real-world examples of successful collaborations that have incorporated AI-powered tools. We will also highlight common challenges and pitfalls to help authors navigate the collaborative writing process and achieve their goals.

Overview of AI-powered tools for collaboration such as Google Docs and Slack

Collaboration is an essential part of the writing and publishing process, and AI-powered tools can make it easier than ever before to work together seamlessly. In this chapter, we'll explore some of the most popular AI-powered collaboration tools available today, including Google Docs and Slack.

Google Docs is a cloud-based word processor that allows multiple users to work on the same document simultaneously. It provides real-time collaboration and commenting features, making it easy for authors and editors to communicate and work together on the same document, no matter where they are located.

Slack, on the other hand, is a messaging and collaboration platform that enables teams to work together in real-time. It provides a variety of channels and direct messaging options, as well as file sharing and integrations with other popular tools.

Both Google Docs and Slack have integrated AI-powered features that can enhance collaboration even further. For example, Google Docs offers Smart Compose, which suggests words and phrases based on the context of what you're writing. Slack has an AI-powered assistant called Slackbot, which can automate repetitive tasks and provide helpful reminders.

Overall, AI-powered collaboration tools like Google

Docs and Slack can save time and improve efficiency in the writing and publishing process. They allow teams to work together seamlessly and provide helpful features that can enhance productivity and creativity. In the next sections, we'll explore some of the best practices for using these tools effectively and efficiently.

Collaboration Tools

1. Google Docs: a cloud-based document editor that allows real-time collaboration, commenting, and revision history tracking.
2. Slack: a messaging platform that enables team communication, file sharing, and project management.
3. Trello: a project management tool that uses boards, cards, and lists to track tasks, deadlines, and progress.
4. Asana: a project management software that allows task management, collaboration, and tracking.
5. Microsoft Teams: a chat-based workspace that integrates with Microsoft Office apps and enables team collaboration, file sharing, and video conferencing.
6. Basecamp: a project management tool that includes to-do lists, scheduling, document sharing, and communication tools.

7. Notion: a workspace and knowledge management tool that allows users to create pages, databases, and wikis to organize and collaborate on information.
8. Airtable: a cloud-based database and collaboration tool that allows users to create custom spreadsheets, calendars, and databases to track information.
9. Dropbox: a cloud-based file sharing and storage platform that allows real-time collaboration on documents, photos, and videos.
10. Zoom: a video conferencing tool that enables virtual meetings, webinars, and screen sharing.

All of these tools offer some level of AI-powered features, such as automated task assignments, chatbots for team communication, and data analysis.

How AI can help authors collaborate with others in the writing process

One of the most significant benefits of using AI-powered collaboration tools is the ability to work on a project in real-time. With tools like Google Docs and Slack, multiple authors can work simultaneously on the same document or project, enabling them to share ideas, feedback, and edits in real-time. This real-time collaboration can save authors significant amounts of time, as they no longer have to wait for others to finish their work before they can begin their own.

Another critical advantage of AI-powered collaboration tools is their ability to improve communication. With features like built-in chat and video conferencing, authors can stay connected with their collaborators and work through any issues or problems that arise in real-time. These tools also provide a central location for all project-related information, including notes, comments, and feedback, making it easier to stay organized and on track.

AI-powered collaboration tools also offer advanced features to support the writing process, including automated proofreading and editing. Tools like Grammarly and ProWritingAid use AI algorithms to analyze text and provide suggestions for improving grammar, spelling, punctuation, and style. This can save authors significant amounts of time and effort by reducing the need for manual proofreading and editing.

Other collaboration tools, such as Hugging Face and OpenAI's GPT-3, provide AI-powered writing assistants that can generate content and help authors overcome writer's block. These tools can suggest ideas and generate content based on keywords or prompts, providing authors with a starting point for their work. These writing assistants can also help authors with research by providing quick access to relevant articles, sources, and data.

It is essential to maintain a balance between AI and

human input to ensure that the final product remains authentic and reflects the authors' voices and perspectives.

AI-powered collaboration tools have transformed the way authors collaborate, providing new tools and capabilities to streamline the process and make it more efficient. With features like real-time collaboration, advanced communication tools, automated proofreading and editing, and AI-powered writing assistants, authors can work more effectively with their collaborators and produce higher quality work in less time.

Examples of how AI-enabled collaboration tools can help in the publishing industry

One example of an AI-powered collaboration tool is the platform Hugging Face. This platform uses AI models to assist in language tasks, making it an ideal tool for collaborative writing projects. By using Hugging Face, collaborators can leverage the power of AI to speed up the writing process and improve the overall quality of the content.

Another example is the writing platform Scrivener. Scrivener includes several AI-powered features that allow collaborators to work more efficiently. For example, its "Name Generator" feature can help writers come up with character names and the "Word Frequency" tool can help identify overused words and phrases.

The platform Novel Factory is another tool that uses AI to support collaboration. Novel Factory's "Character Profile

Generator" feature uses AI algorithms to create detailed character profiles, which can be useful for collaborative worldbuilding.

AI-powered collaboration tools have also been used to streamline the editing and proofreading process. One example is the platform Grammarly, which uses AI to check grammar and spelling errors. By using Grammarly, editors and proofreaders can save time and improve the overall accuracy of the content.

Another example is the platform ProWritingAid, which uses AI algorithms to provide suggestions for improving sentence structure, vocabulary, and other writing elements. This tool can be particularly useful for collaborative editing projects, as it provides clear and actionable feedback to authors and editors.

Finally, the platform Inkitt uses AI to provide insights into readers' preferences and behaviors. By using Inkitt, publishers can gain valuable insights into the marketability of their work, which can inform collaborative decision-making around marketing and distribution.

AI-powered collaboration tools have transformed the writing and publishing industry, providing authors, editors, and publishers with new and innovative ways to work together. These tools have the potential to increase efficiency, improve quality, and streamline the overall publishing process. As such, it is important for authors and publishers to explore the possibilities of these AI-powered tools and incorporate them into their collaborative workflows.

Best practices for using AI tools for collaboration

We have found there are several best practices to keep in mind to ensure collaboration tools are used effectively and responsibly.

1. Clearly define roles and responsibilities: It is essential to establish clear roles and responsibilities for each team member involved in the collaboration process. This includes defining who will be responsible for creating and managing the AI-generated content, as well as who will be responsible for editing and proofreading the content. Establishing clear roles and responsibilities will help ensure that everyone is on the same page and working towards a common goal.

2. Choose the right tool for the job: With so many AI-powered collaboration tools available, it is important to choose the right tool for the task at hand. Consider factors such as the type of content being created, the size of the team, and the level of collaboration required. For example, if the team is small and working on a single document, a tool like

Google Docs may be sufficient. However, if the team is larger and working on multiple documents, a tool like Asana may be more appropriate.

3. Set clear goals and deadlines: Setting clear goals and deadlines is essential for any collaboration effort, and using AI tools is no exception. Establishing specific goals and deadlines can help ensure that everyone is working towards the same objectives and can help keep the team on track. It is important to communicate these goals and deadlines clearly and regularly to ensure that everyone is aware of the timeline and what is expected of them.

4. Ensure data privacy and security: When using AI tools for collaboration, it is essential to ensure that data privacy and security are maintained. This includes ensuring sensitive information is not shared with unauthorized parties, and that all team members are aware of their responsibilities regarding data security. It may be necessary to use secure communication channels, such as encrypted messaging platforms, to ensure that sensitive information is protected.

5. Stay aware of ethical considerations: As with any use of AI, it is essential to stay aware of ethical considerations when using AI tools for collaboration. This includes ensuring the use of AI tools does not result in bias or discrimination,

and that the content produced is not misleading or harmful in any way. Regularly reviewing and analyzing the content produced by AI tools can help ensure that these ethical considerations are being met.

Real-world examples of best practices for using AI tools for collaboration can be seen in the work of companies such as OpenAI and IBM Watson. OpenAI's GPT-3 language model has been used in a variety of collaboration efforts, including creating chatbots and generating creative writing content. IBM Watson has been used in collaborative efforts to generate legal briefs and analyze medical data.

By following best practices such as defining clear roles and responsibilities, choosing the right tool for the job, setting clear goals and deadlines, ensuring data privacy and security, and staying aware of ethical considerations, authors can ensure that their collaboration efforts are successful and produce high-quality content.

CHAPTER 7
CREATIVE INSPIRATION

As writing is a creative process, it can be challenging to come up with new and innovative ideas. However, AI-powered tools can help authors break through creative blocks and generate fresh ideas.

We wanted to spend some time discussing the various ways in which AI can support creative inspiration, including generating prompts and ideas, providing research assistance, and enhancing creativity through machine learning algorithms.

Additionally, we'll cover the need to maintain authenticity and originality in writing. Ultimately, this chapter aims to provide authors with a comprehensive understanding of how AI can be used to enhance their creative process and generate fresh ideas for their writing projects.

Overview of AI-powered tools for creative inspiration such as Artbreeder and DALL·E

AI-powered tools for creative inspiration offer authors and creators a wide range of possibilities to explore their imagination and artistic vision. These tools use machine learning algorithms to generate unique and innovative visual and textual outputs, providing endless sources of inspiration for writers.

One such tool is Artbreeder, which allows users to combine and mutate different images to generate new, unique visuals. With a user-friendly interface, Artbreeder offers authors the chance to create custom cover art, character illustrations, and even settings for their stories.

Another powerful tool is DALL·E, which generates images from text descriptions. This cutting-edge tool uses a state-of-the-art neural network to translate textual prompts into striking visual images. Authors can use DALL·E to generate high-quality, unique illustrations for their stories, or even create visuals for marketing materials.

For writers looking to explore new ideas and stretch their creativity, AI-powered tools like Artbreeder and DALL·E offer a wealth of possibilities. These tools can be especially helpful for writers who struggle with artist's block or those looking to push their creative boundaries in new directions.

By using these tools, authors can add a unique touch to their writing and stand out in a crowded market. The possibilities are endless, and the only limit is the author's imagination.

However, while using AI-powered tools for creative inspiration can be highly beneficial, there are also ethical considerations to keep in mind. It's important for authors to use these tools in a responsible manner and to ensure that any images or content generated through these tools do not infringe on intellectual property rights.

As with any tool, it's also crucial to maintain a balance between the use of AI-generated content and authentic, original content. Authors should use these tools to enhance their work, not to replace their own creativity and unique perspective.

Creative Inspiration Tools

1. Artbreeder: This tool uses GANs to generate unique, high-quality images that can be used as inspiration for writing. Users can mix and match different traits to create a one-of-a-kind image.
2. DALL·E: This tool was created by OpenAI and uses GPT-3 to generate images based on text descriptions. Users can input a description and the tool will generate an image that matches it.
3. Canva: This tool provides a wide variety of templates and designs that can be used for inspiration. Users can browse through templates and modify them to fit their needs.

4. Midjourney: This tool uses AI to generate ideas for creative projects. Users input a description of their project and the tool generates a list of ideas to help get the creative juices flowing.

5. The Brainstormer: This tool provides a random combination of three elements to inspire creativity. Users can spin the wheel to generate a new combination of elements.

While these tools can be useful for sparking creativity and generating ideas, it is important to remember that they are just tools. The role of human creativity is still critical in the creative process. AI-generated images and concepts should be used as a starting point for creativity and should be modified and adapted to fit the author's unique vision.

It's important to consider any potential copyright or legal issues that may arise. AI-generated images and concepts may still be subject to copyright laws, and it is important to ensure the use of these images is in compliance with these laws.

How AI can help authors find visual and conceptual ideas for their writing

AI has the potential to assist authors in finding creative inspiration for their writing. AI-powered tools such as Artbreeder, DALL·E, and Midjourney can help authors generate visual and conceptual ideas that may lead to unique and innovative storylines.

Midjourney is another AI-powered tool that helps authors find visual inspiration for their writing. It uses machine learning to analyze images and generate a set of related images. By selecting an image that speaks to them, authors can discover new and unexpected ideas for their writing.

These AI-powered tools can also assist authors in overcoming writer's block by providing new ideas. When an author is struggling, they can turn to these tools to generate inspiration and creativity.

AI-powered tools for creative inspiration such as Artbreeder, DALL·E, and Midjourney can be valuable resources for authors looking to find visual and conceptual inspiration for their writing. However, authors should be mindful of their use and ensure that they are being used in conjunction with their own creativity and originality.

How to use AI-generated images and concepts in a way that is unique and original

AI-generated images and concepts can be incredibly helpful to authors seeking visual inspiration for their writing. However, it is important to use these resources in a way that is unique and original. Here are some best practices for using AI-generated images and concepts in your writing:

1. Use them as a starting point: Rather than relying solely on AI-generated images and concepts, use them as a starting point to generate your own unique ideas. Take the inspiration provided by these tools and build upon it with your own creativity.

2. Combine multiple sources: Don't limit yourself to just one AI-generated image or concept. Use multiple sources and combine them in interesting ways to create something truly unique.

3. Customize the image or concept: Many AI-generated images and concepts are highly customizable. Use these tools to tweak the details and create something that is truly your own.

4. Incorporate your own style: Don't be afraid to incorporate your own personal style into the AI-generated images and concepts you use. This will help make them feel more original and unique to your writing.

5. Avoid direct replication: While AI-generated images and concepts can be incredibly helpful for inspiration, it is important to avoid directly replicating them. Always think of them as a starting point.

The use of AI-generated images and concepts in a way that is unique and original may present some copyright and legal ramifications, particularly if the images or concepts are created using copyrighted material or infringe on intellectual property rights. It is important to ensure that any AI-generated images or concepts used in your work do not violate any copyright laws or infringe on the rights of others.

One potential solution is to use AI-powered tools that allow you to manipulate and alter images or concepts in a way that transforms them into something new and original. For example, the use of Artbreeder to generate a base image that is then manipulated and altered by the author to create something unique and original would likely not pose a copyright or legal issue.

It is also important to conduct thorough research and due diligence when using AI-generated images or concepts, particularly if they are intended for commercial use or publication. Ensuring that the images or concepts used are free of copyright or intellectual property violations can help protect against potential legal issues.

The role of human creativity in combination with AI in the creative inspiration process

As much as AI-powered tools for creative inspiration can be powerful resources for authors, they cannot replace human creativity. In fact, the combination of human and AI creativity can result in even more unique and compelling ideas.

AI can be used to generate a wide range of visual and conceptual ideas, but it is up to the author to take those ideas and shape them into something that is truly their own. It is important to not rely too heavily on AI-generated concepts and images, but to use them as a starting point for further exploration and development.

Human creativity can add a level of nuance and complexity to AI-generated ideas that can make them stand out and feel more authentic. For example, an AI-generated character design could be further developed by a human author to include specific personality traits and backstory that give the character depth and emotional resonance.

By combining AI-generated ideas with human creativity, authors can create something truly unique and original. It is important to remember that AI is a tool to aid in the creative process, not a replacement for it.

Ultimately, the role of human creativity in combination with AI in the creative inspiration process is to add a layer of authenticity and originality to AI-generated ideas. By doing so, authors can create truly unique and compelling works of art.

CHAPTER 8
EDITING AND PROOFREADING

E diting and proofreading are essential steps in the writing process. Even the most skilled writers can make mistakes, and having errors in your work can diminish the impact of your writing. Fortunately, AI-powered tools can help authors to edit and proofread their work more efficiently and accurately. In this chapter, we will explore the different ways that AI can assist authors in the editing and proofreading process.

Editing is a crucial part of the writing process, but it can also be time-consuming and tedious. Fortunately, AI-powered tools can help streamline and automate many aspects of the editing process, from grammar and syntax to style and tone.

In this chapter, we will explore the various ways in which AI tools can support authors in editing their work. We will provide an overview of the editing process, and then delve into specific AI-powered tools that can assist with grammar, syntax, style, tone, and more.

We will also discuss the ethical considerations surrounding the use of AI in editing, such as the importance of preserving the author's voice and style, as well as the potential risks of over-reliance on AI-generated suggestions.

Overall, this chapter will provide valuable insights and practical advice for authors looking to use AI tools to enhance their editing process and improve the quality of their writing.

Overview of AI-powered tools for editing and proofreading such as Grammarly, Hemingway, and ProWritingAid

AI-powered editing and proofreading tools have become increasingly popular among writers, editors, and publishers alike. These tools not only help to correct errors in grammar, spelling, and punctuation, but they can also provide valuable insights into style and readability. Here is an overview of some of the top AI-powered editing and proofreading tools:

1. Grammarly - Perhaps the most well-known editing tool on the market, Grammarly uses AI to identify and correct over 400 types of grammatical errors. It also provides suggestions for improving clarity, conciseness, and tone.

2. Hemingway - This tool analyzes your writing for readability, identifying areas where you can simplify your language, eliminate unnecessary words, and improve sentence structure. It also highlights adverbs, passive voice, and other elements that can weaken your writing.

3. ProWritingAid - In addition to basic grammar and spelling checks, ProWritingAid offers advanced editing tools that analyze your writing for issues such as repeated words and phrases, inconsistent tenses, and overuse of adverbs.

4. Ginger - Similar to Grammarly, Ginger checks for grammar and spelling errors and provides suggestions for improving your writing. It also includes a feature that allows you to rephrase sentences to avoid plagiarism.

5. WhiteSmoke - This tool offers both grammar and style checking, analyzing your writing for issues such as sentence structure, word choice, and punctuation. It also includes a translator and a plagiarism checker.

6. LanguageTool - This open-source tool checks for grammar, spelling, and punctuation errors in over 20 languages. It also offers suggestions for improving your writing style and tone.

7. Typely - This tool provides a minimalist interface that allows you to focus on your writing. It checks for grammar and spelling

errors, as well as issues such as passive voice and cliches.

8. AutoCrit - Designed specifically for fiction writers, AutoCrit analyzes your writing for issues such as pacing, dialogue, and repetition. It also includes a tool for generating book summaries and synopses.

9. Prose Media - This AI-powered writing platform offers editing and proofreading services from a team of human editors. The platform uses AI to match you with an editor who has expertise in your specific genre.

10. Scribendi - Another platform that offers human editing services, Scribendi uses AI to analyze your writing and match you with an editor who can provide targeted feedback and suggestions for improvement.

11. Overall, AI-powered editing and proofreading tools can be a valuable resource for writers and editors, helping to improve the quality of their writing and streamline the editing process.

12. ProWritingAid: ProWritingAid is an AI-powered editing tool that helps writers to improve their writing style, grammar, and spelling. It can be used as a standalone application or as a browser extension.

13. Autocrit: Autocrit is an AI-powered editing tool that helps writers to identify weaknesses in their

writing, such as overused words and passive voice. It also provides suggestions for how to improve your writing.

14. Wordtune: Wordtune is an AI-powered writing tool that helps writers to improve their writing by suggesting alternative words and phrases. It can be used as a browser extension or as a standalone application.

How AI can help authors improve the quality of their writing

One way AI can help authors improve the quality of their writing is by identifying common errors and providing suggestions for corrections. For example, Grammarly is an AI-powered editing tool that can identify grammatical and punctuation errors in your writing and offer suggestions for correction. Hemingway, another popular editing tool, can help you to simplify your writing and improve its readability by highlighting complex sentences and identifying areas where you can use simpler language.

Another way AI can help authors improve the quality of their writing is by analyzing the style and tone of their writing. ProWritingAid, for instance, is an AI-powered editing tool that can identify overused words and phrases, cliches, and other stylistic issues in your writing. It can also analyze your writing for tone, helping you to ensure that your writing is appropriately formal, casual, or professional depending on your intended audience.

AI can also assist with improving the overall structure and organization of your writing. For example, the AI-powered tool QuillBot can help to generate alternate sentence structures and paraphrase complex sentences to help improve clarity and readability. This can be especially useful for writers who are struggling to find the right words or phrasing to express their ideas.

Real-life examples of how AI-powered editing tools have been used in the publishing industry

AI-powered editing tools have been used in the publishing industry to help authors and editors improve the quality of their writing. Here are some real-life examples:

1. The New York Times: The New York Times uses an AI-powered tool called Editor to help with the editing process. The tool checks for spelling and grammar errors, as well as offering suggestions for improving style and structure.
2. Wired: Wired magazine used Grammarly, an AI-powered writing assistant, to edit and proofread their articles. The tool helped catch errors and suggested improvements to the writing style.
3. The Wall Street Journal: The Wall Street Journal uses an AI-powered editing tool called Tansa to

help with proofreading. The tool checks for errors in spelling, grammar, and punctuation, and suggests corrections.

4. Forbes: Forbes magazine used an AI-powered writing assistant called Atomic Reach to improve their writing. The tool offered suggestions for improving readability, tone, and style.

5. The Guardian: The Guardian newspaper used an AI-powered editing tool called Sub-Edit to help with the editing process. The tool checks for errors in spelling, grammar, and punctuation, and suggests corrections.

6. The Associated Press: The Associated Press uses an AI-powered tool called Wordsmith to help with automated news writing. The tool generates articles based on data and templates, allowing for fast and efficient article production.

7. The Los Angeles Times: The Los Angeles Times uses an AI-powered tool called Utopia to help with editing and proofreading. The tool checks for errors in spelling, grammar, and punctuation, and suggests corrections.

Reference: "How Artificial Intelligence is Helping Newsrooms Improve Workflow and Quality" by AI in News, https://www.ai-in.news/en/how-artificial-intelligence-is-helping-

newsrooms-improve-workflow-and-quality/ (accessed August 17, 2021)

THESE EXAMPLES DEMONSTRATE the diverse range of AI-powered editing tools available in the publishing industry and how they can improve the quality of writing for different media outlets.

Best practices for using AI tools for editing and proofreading

Here are some best practices for using AI tools for editing and proofreading:

1. Understand the limitations of AI: AI tools are not perfect and can make mistakes, especially when it comes to grammar and language nuances. Always use your own judgment to evaluate the suggestions made by the tool.
2. Use multiple tools: It's a good idea to use multiple AI-powered editing tools to catch as many errors as possible. Different tools use different algorithms and have different strengths and weaknesses.
3. Use the right tool for the right purpose: Different tools are designed for different purposes, such as grammar checking, spelling checking, or style

checking. Make sure you're using the right tool for the specific type of editing or proofreading you need.

4. Adjust the settings: Many AI-powered editing tools allow you to adjust the settings to better suit your needs. For example, you may be able to adjust the sensitivity of the tool to catch more or fewer errors.

5. Use in combination with human editors: While AI-powered editing tools can be a valuable tool in the editing and proofreading process, they should not replace human editors entirely. Consider using the tools in combination with human editors to get the best results.

6. Train the tool: Some AI-powered editing tools allow you to train the tool to better understand your writing style and preferences. Take advantage of this feature to get more accurate suggestions.

7. Keep learning: AI-powered editing tools are constantly improving and evolving. Stay up to date with the latest tools and features to make the most of their potential.

PART III
PUBLISHING

Part 2: PUBLISHING is dedicated to exploring the ways in which AI can revolutionize the publishing process. From the moment an author puts the finishing touches on a manuscript to the point at which the book is marketed to potential readers, AI can be an invaluable tool for improving the efficiency and effectiveness of the publishing process.

The chapters in this section will explore the ways in which AI can be used to streamline publishing workflows, enhance the accuracy of book metadata, and support targeted marketing efforts. By leveraging the power of AI, publishers can make the most of their resources, while ensuring their books reach the widest possible audience.

Whether you are an independent author looking to self-publish your first book, or a seasoned publishing professional working for a major publishing house, this section will provide you with the knowledge and tools you need to succeed in the rapidly-evolving world of AI-powered publishing.

Roadmap to Publishing with AI

I. Acquiring the Manuscript

- Use AI-powered tools such as AI Book Scout or Biblioso to scan through large volumes of unpublished manuscripts and identify potential works that fit the publisher's criteria.
- AI-powered language analysis tools like Textio can help in identifying manuscripts with strong writing style and story structure.

II. Editing and Proofreading

- Use AI-powered grammar checkers like Grammarly or ProWritingAid to quickly identify and correct grammar and spelling mistakes.
- AI-powered editing tools like Prose Media can assist with substantive editing, ensuring the manuscript is well-structured and free of plot holes.

- AI-powered proofreading tools like PerfectIt can help to ensure consistent formatting and citation style across the manuscript.

III. Design and Layout

- AI-powered design tools like Canva can help to create eye-catching cover designs.
- AI-powered layout tools like Vellum can assist in formatting the manuscript for digital or print publication.

IV. Marketing and Promotion

- AI-powered marketing analytics tools like Parse.ly or SEMrush can help to identify target audiences and track the performance of marketing campaigns.
- AI-powered chatbots like Octane AI or Tars can be used to engage with potential readers on social media and provide personalized recommendations based on their interests.
- AI-powered ad creation tools like Albert can help to create and optimize ad campaigns across multiple channels.

V. Distribution

- AI-powered distribution platforms like PublishDrive can assist in distributing the novel to various online retailers and libraries worldwide.

VI. Sales Analysis and Optimization

- AI-powered sales analysis tools like BookData or NovelRank can provide detailed sales data and insights, helping publishers to optimize pricing and marketing strategies.

CHAPTER 9
DATA ANALYSIS AND INSIGHTS

Data analysis and insights are important to authors because they provide valuable information that can help authors make informed decisions about their writing and publishing strategies. By analyzing data such as book sales, reader behavior, and market trends, authors can gain insights into what types of books are popular, what readers are looking for, and how to better position their own books in the market.

For example, data analysis can help authors identify trends in the book market and adjust their writing or marketing strategies accordingly. It can also help authors understand which promotional channels are most effective and which readers are most engaged with their work. By tracking data and analyzing insights, authors can make data-driven decisions about everything from book pricing to cover design to promotional strategies.

Additionally, data analysis can help authors better understand their own writing style and strengths, as well as areas where they may need to improve. By tracking data on the readability of their writing or the types of words and phrases they use most frequently, authors can gain insights into how to improve their craft and better engage readers.

Overall, data analysis and insights are a valuable tool for authors in today's publishing landscape, helping them to stay competitive and make informed decisions about their writing and publishing strategies.

This chapter delves into how AI can be used in the publishing industry for data analysis and insights. We will explore how authors and publishers can use AI-powered tools to gain a deeper understanding of their audience and market trends. By analyzing data and gaining insights, authors can make informed decisions about their writing and publishing strategy.

We will provide an overview of AI-powered tools for data analysis and insights, such as Google Analytics and K-lytics, and discuss how they can be used to analyze data related to book sales, reader demographics, and market trends. We will also explore how these tools can be used to analyze social media and website traffic to gain insights into reader behavior and preferences.

In addition, we will examine the ethical considerations surrounding the use of data analysis and insights in the publishing industry. We will discuss how to use data responsibly and avoid biases in analysis. We will also explore how data analysis can be used to enhance diversity and inclusion in publishing.

Overview of AI-powered tools for data analysis and insights such as Bookstat, PublishDrive, and Amazon KDP reports

One of the key benefits of AI-powered data analysis tools is their ability to process large amounts of data quickly and accurately. This means authors can gather insights on their books and their audience without spending hours manually analyzing sales data or reviews.

Bookstat, for example, is a tool that provides real-time sales data for books across various online retailers. This allows authors to monitor their sales and identify trends that can inform their marketing and promotional efforts. PublishDrive is another tool that provides authors with sales and performance data across multiple platforms, including Amazon, Barnes & Noble, and Apple Books. These insights can help authors make informed decisions about pricing, advertising, and distribution.

Amazon KDP reports, meanwhile, is a free tool provided by Amazon to self-published authors. It allows authors to track their book's sales and performance data, including royalties earned, page reads, and customer reviews.

Other AI-powered tools for data analysis and insights include Reedsy Insights, a platform that provides authors with market intelligence and publishing trends, and Google Analytics, a tool that tracks website traffic and user behavior.

Sample Tools

Here is a list of sample AI data analysis tools for authors and a brief description of each:

1. Bookstat - A tool that provides real-time data analysis on book sales across various online platforms, including Amazon, Barnes & Noble, and Apple Books.

2. PublishDrive - A platform that offers comprehensive data analysis tools for ebook distribution, including sales tracking, market research, and promotional insights.

3. Amazon KDP Reports - Amazon's proprietary data analysis tool for self-published authors, which provides detailed sales data, including sales trends and customer feedback.

4. BookBub - A book discovery platform that offers insights into book sales and marketing trends, including genre-specific data and reader engagement metrics.

5. Reedsy Discovery - A platform that connects authors with professional reviewers and offers data analysis tools to help authors understand reader engagement and discoverability.

6. Writer's Digest - A resource for writers that provides insights into industry trends, publishing news, and marketing strategies based on data analysis.

7. Prose Media - A content marketing agency that offers data analysis tools to help authors and publishers optimize their marketing campaigns and increase book sales.

8. K-lytics - A tool that provides insights into the ebook market, including genre-specific data, reader demographics, and keyword analysis.

9. Hiptype - A data analytics platform for publishers that offers insights into reader behavior, including which parts of the book are being read and how readers are engaging with the content.

10. BookReport - A data analysis tool that provides sales insights, reader engagement metrics, and competitor analysis for self-published authors.

How AI can help authors track and analyze book sales, reader behavior, and market trends

As the publishing industry becomes increasingly data-driven, authors are turning to AI-powered tools to track and analyze book sales, reader behavior, and market trends. AI can provide authors with valuable insights that can help them make informed decisions about their writing and marketing strategies.

One way AI can help authors track their book sales is by analyzing sales data and identifying patterns and trends. For example, Amazon KDP reports can provide authors with detailed sales data, including the number of units sold, royalties earned, and customer demographics. AI-powered tools such as Bookstat and PublishDrive can also help authors track their sales data and provide detailed reports on sales performance.

In addition to sales data, AI can also help authors track reader behavior and engagement. Tools like BookBub Ads and Book Brush can help authors create targeted advertising campaigns and track reader engagement metrics such as click-through rates and conversion rates.

AI can also be used to analyze market trends and identify new opportunities for authors. For example, AI-powered tools like AuthorEarnings and K-Lytics can analyze market data and provide authors with insights into popular genres and subgenres, as well as emerging trends and niches.

Overall, the use of AI-powered data analysis tools can help authors make informed decisions about their writing and marketing strategies.

Real-life examples of how AI-powered data analysis tools have been used in the publishing industry

Here are some real-life examples of how AI-powered data analysis tools have been used in the publishing industry:

1. Hachette Book Group: Hachette Book Group used data analytics to identify books that were likely to be bestsellers. They analyzed data on reader behavior and sales trends to make informed decisions on which books to acquire and promote.

2. HarperCollins Publishers: HarperCollins Publishers used AI-powered data analysis tools to optimize their book covers for maximum impact. They analyzed reader behavior and market trends to determine which design elements were most effective in attracting readers.

3. Amazon Publishing: Amazon Publishing uses AI-powered data analysis tools to identify niche audiences and tailor their marketing efforts to those audiences. They analyze data on reader behavior and sales trends to identify specific demographics that are likely to be interested in a particular book.

4. Penguin Random House: Penguin Random House uses AI-powered data analysis tools to analyze reader behavior and optimize their

marketing efforts. They use machine learning algorithms to analyze reader reviews and identify trends in reader preferences, which they use to inform their marketing strategy.

5. Wattpad: Wattpad uses AI-powered data analysis tools to identify popular topics and genres, and to help authors tailor their writing to those topics and genres. They analyze reader behavior and engagement metrics to determine which types of content are most popular and which topics are likely to be successful.

BIBLIOGRAPHY

Hachette Book Group: https://www.hachettebookgroup.com/

Forbes: https://www.forbes.com/

Publishers Weekly: https://www.publishersweekly.com/

HarperCollins Publishers: https://www.harpercollins.com/

Amazon Publishing: https://www.amazon.com/gp/browse.html?node=16522225011

Penguin Random House: https://www.penguinrandomhouse.com/

Wattpad: https://www.wattpad.com/

. . .

AI-POWERED DATA ANALYSIS TOOLS: https://www.wattpad.com/press/2020/4/21/wattpad-launches-ai-powered-data-analytics-tools-for-publishers-authors-and-literary-agents/

THESE EXAMPLES SHOW how AI-powered data analysis tools are being used by publishers to make data-driven decisions and optimize their marketing efforts. By analyzing data on reader behavior, sales trends, and market preferences, publishers can make more informed decisions on which books to acquire, promote, and market, and can tailor their marketing efforts to specific audiences for maximum impact.

Best practices for using AI tools for data analysis and insights

1. Set clear goals: Before using any AI tool, it's important to define what you want to achieve. Identify the key metrics you want to track, such as sales, reader engagement, or marketing performance, and make sure you have a clear understanding of the insights you want to gain.
2. Choose the right tools: There are many AI-powered data analysis tools available, each with different capabilities and features. Take the time to research and compare different options to find the tool that best fits your needs. AI4A provides

support in this area helping our customers find just the right tools for the job.

3. Verify data accuracy: While AI tools can provide valuable insights, it's important to ensure that the data you are analyzing is accurate. Check the data sources and make sure the information is reliable and up-to-date.

4. Use data to inform decisions: Once you have collected and analyzed your data, use the insights gained to inform your decision-making. This can include making changes to your marketing strategy, adjusting your pricing, or identifying new target audiences.

5. Keep learning: AI tools are constantly evolving, so it's important to stay up-to-date on the latest developments and new features. Attend webinars, read blogs, and engage with other authors and publishers to learn about new tools and techniques. AI4A has built a community to foster shared knowledge.

CHAPTER 10
AI AND BOOK DISCOVERY

Discovery of books is a vital aspect of the publishing industry, serving as a key tool for authors and publishers to expand their readership and generate buzz around their works. AI-powered tools for book discovery, such as Goodreads and BookBub, can help in the following ways:

1. Audience targeting: By using AI algorithms, these tools can identify and target specific reader demographics based on their reading habits, preferences, and ratings. This helps authors and publishers to reach their target audience and increase the chances of book discovery.

2. Book recommendations: AI-powered book discovery tools can also recommend books to readers based on their reading history, ratings,

and reviews. This can lead to increased visibility and exposure for authors and their books.

3. Promotion: Many AI-powered book discovery tools also offer promotional opportunities for authors and publishers, such as advertising or book deals. This can help boost book sales and increase visibility among potential readers.

4. Data analysis: AI-powered tools can also provide data insights into reader behavior, such as which books are being read the most, what genres are popular, and how long readers are spending on certain books. This data can help authors and publishers make informed decisions about book marketing and promotion strategies.

Overall, book discovery with AI-powered tools can be a valuable resource for authors and publishers looking to increase the visibility of their books and reach a wider audience.

The world of book discovery is changing rapidly, and AI is playing a major role in this transformation. This chapter will explore the ways in which AI-powered tools can help authors and publishers improve book discoverability and connect with readers.

We will provide an overview of AI-powered tools for book discovery, including platforms like Amazon's recommendation engine, Goodreads, and BookBub. We will also examine how AI can be used to optimize metadata, book descriptions, and cover design to improve discoverability.

Overview of AI-powered tools for book discovery such as Goodreads and BookBub

In recent years, book discovery has become a crucial aspect of the publishing industry. With so many books being published each year, it can be difficult for authors to get their work noticed by potential readers. Fortunately, AI-powered tools have emerged to help authors with book discovery.

Goodreads is one such tool that has become increasingly popular. It is a social network for book lovers that allows users to rate and review books, create reading lists, and connect with other readers. Goodreads uses AI algorithms to suggest books to users based on their reading history and preferences. For authors, having a presence on Goodreads can help them reach a wider audience and gain valuable insights into reader preferences.

BookBub is another popular tool for book discovery. It is a platform that connects readers with limited-time deals on ebooks. BookBub uses AI algorithms to send personalized recommendations to its subscribers based on their reading history and preferences. Authors can use BookBub to promote their books and reach a wider audience.

Other AI-powered book discovery tools include K-lytics, which provides insights into the bestselling categories and keywords on Amazon, and Reedsy Discovery, which allows readers to discover new books and provides authors with a platform to promote their work.

With the help of AI-powered book discovery tools, authors can increase their visibility and reach a wider audience.

How AI can help authors discover new books and compare their books to other authors

As an author, it's important to stay up to date on current trends and to be aware of what other authors are writing. However, keeping track of all the books out there can be a daunting task. This is where AI-powered book discovery tools come in handy. These tools use algorithms to analyze user data and suggest books based on user preferences and behavior. Here are some ways in which AI can help authors discover new books and compare their books to other authors:

1. Recommending similar books: AI-powered book discovery tools analyze reader behavior and suggest similar books based on user preferences. This can help authors find books that are similar to their own and get ideas for their own writing.

2. Identifying market trends: AI-powered tools can analyze sales data and identify market trends, allowing authors to make more informed

decisions about their own work. For example, if a certain genre is gaining popularity, an author may want to consider writing in that genre.

3. Analyzing author profiles: AI-powered tools can analyze author profiles and identify similar authors based on writing style, genre, and other factors. This can help authors find other writers to collaborate with or simply gain inspiration from.

4. Generating keyword ideas: AI-powered tools can analyze user search queries and generate keyword ideas for authors to use in their book descriptions and metadata. This can help improve the discoverability of an author's work.

5. Predicting sales: AI-powered sales prediction tools can analyze book metadata and sales data to predict how well a book will sell. This can help authors make more informed decisions about marketing and advertising.

Overall, AI-powered book discovery tools can help authors stay up to date on current trends, find inspiration for their writing, and make more informed decisions about their work. By using these tools, authors can stay ahead of the curve and increase their chances of success in the competitive publishing industry.

AI-powered Book Discovery Tools

Here is a list of some AI-powered tools that can help authors discover new books and compare their books to other authors:

1. Goodreads - Goodreads is a social cataloging website that allows users to search for and discover new books. The site also provides book recommendations based on users' reading history and ratings.
2. BookBub - BookBub is a website that provides readers with daily deals on e-books. The site uses AI algorithms to provide personalized book recommendations based on users' reading preferences.
3. Amazon Author Central - Amazon Author Central is a platform for authors to manage their Amazon book listings and track their sales. The platform provides authors with data on their book sales, including information on their book's ranking and reviews.
4. Reedsy Discovery - Reedsy Discovery is a platform that helps authors discover new books and get their books discovered by readers. The platform provides personalized book recommendations based on users' reading preferences and also allows authors to submit

their books for review by a team of professional reviewers.

5. PubMatch - PubMatch is a platform that connects authors, publishers, and literary agents. The platform provides authors with a way to discover new publishing opportunities and to showcase their work to potential publishers and agents.

6. BookLens - BookLens is an AI-powered tool that provides personalized book recommendations based on users' reading habits and preferences. The tool uses natural language processing and machine learning algorithms to analyze books and make recommendations to users.

7. Writerly - Writerly is an AI-powered tool that allows authors to compare their writing style to other authors in their genre. The tool provides authors with insights into their writing style and helps them identify areas for improvement.

8. BookRank - BookRank is a tool that allows authors to track their book's performance on Amazon. The tool provides authors with real-time data on their book's ranking, sales, and reviews, as well as insights into their book's performance relative to other books in their genre.

The potential impact of AI on the book discovery process and the publishing industry

The impact of AI on the book discovery process and the publishing industry has been significant in recent years. AI-powered book discovery tools have changed the way readers find and select books to read, and they have also provided authors and publishers with valuable insights into reader behavior and preferences.

One of the most significant impacts of AI on the book discovery process is the ability to personalize book recommendations for readers. By analyzing a reader's past reading habits, AI-powered tools can recommend books that are more likely to interest them. This has led to a more efficient book discovery process and has helped readers discover books that they may not have otherwise found.

Additionally, AI-powered book discovery tools have given authors and publishers valuable insights into reader behavior and preferences. By analyzing data on which books are being read, which genres are popular, and other factors, authors and publishers can make more informed decisions about which books to publish and how to market them.

However, there are also concerns about the potential impact of AI on the publishing industry. Some experts worry that AI-powered book discovery tools could lead to a homogenization of the book market, with publishers and authors only producing books that fit within certain popular genres and formulas.

Furthermore, there is concern about the role of AI in selecting which books get published and promoted. If AI tools are used to select books based solely on marketability, there is a risk that innovative or experimental works may be overlooked in favor of more formulaic, commercially successful books.

Overall, while AI-powered book discovery tools have brought significant benefits to the publishing industry, there are also concerns about their potential impact. It is important for authors, publishers, and readers to carefully consider the role of AI in the book discovery process and to ensure that it is used in a way that promotes creativity, diversity, and innovation in the publishing industry.

CHAPTER 11
BOOK PROMOTION

This chapter focuses on how authors can use AI to promote and market their books. With so many books available, it's essential to have a well-planned marketing strategy to reach your target audience and stand out in the crowd. In this chapter, we explore the various AI-powered tools that can help authors develop and execute effective book promotion and marketing campaigns.

We begin by discussing the importance of identifying and understanding your target audience, and how AI can assist in this process. We then delve into the different ways that AI can be used to promote your book, including email marketing, social media advertising, and content marketing. We also explore the role of AI in data-driven marketing, and how it can be used to optimize your campaigns and improve your ROI.

Throughout the chapter, we provide real-life examples of how AI-powered marketing tools have been used in the publishing industry. We also discuss the potential impact of AI on book promotion and marketing, and how it is likely to shape the future of the publishing industry.

Overview of AI-powered tools for book promotion such as social media management, email marketing, and book advertising tools

AI-powered tools for book promotion include social media management, email marketing, and book advertising tools that can help authors effectively market their books to a wider audience.

Social media management tools like Hootsuite and Buffer allow authors to schedule and manage their social media posts across multiple platforms. These tools use AI algorithms to suggest the best times to post based on audience engagement and provide analytics to track the success of the posts.

Email marketing tools like Mailchimp and Constant Contact can help authors build and manage their email lists, create visually appealing emails, and track open and click-through rates. These tools also use AI algorithms to personalize emails based on reader preferences and behaviors.

Book advertising tools like BookBub Ads and Amazon Ads allow authors to create targeted advertising campaigns based on reader demographics, interests, and search history. These tools use AI algorithms to optimize ad performance and suggest the best targeting options for maximum reach and engagement.

Other AI-powered book promotion tools include:

- Reedsy Promotions: a platform that helps authors find book promotion services and tools that fit their needs and budget, using AI algorithms to match authors with the best options.
- DataCaptive: a tool that uses AI algorithms to create targeted contact lists for book promotion, based on reader demographics and interests.
- Snipfeed: a platform that uses AI algorithms to match readers with books they are likely to enjoy, based on their reading preferences and behaviors.
- Book Blaster: a book promotion tool that uses AI to target readers with personalized book recommendations.

These tools can save authors time and effort in promoting their books, while also providing valuable data and insights to optimize their marketing strategies.

How AI can help authors reach a wider audience and increase book sales

AI can play a significant role in helping authors reach a wider audience and increase book sales. With the ever-increasing amount of content being produced, it's becoming increasingly challenging to stand out in the crowded market-place. AI-powered tools can help authors to create more targeted and effective marketing campaigns that will get their books in front of the right readers.

One way AI can help authors reach a wider audience is through social media management. AI tools can analyze social media data to identify the most effective posting times and types of content for specific audiences. By utilizing these insights, authors can create social media campaigns that are tailored to their target audience, leading to more engagement, followers, and ultimately more book sales.

Another way AI can help authors reach a wider audience is through email marketing. AI-powered email marketing tools can analyze data on subscriber behavior to create personalized email campaigns that are more likely to be opened and engaged with. These tools can also analyze email performance data to optimize campaigns for better results, leading to increased book sales.

AI can also be used to target book advertising campaigns more effectively. With the help of AI-powered tools, authors can identify and target audiences that are more likely to be interested in their books. This can be done through the use of data analysis, which can reveal insights into reader demographics and preferences.

In addition to the above, AI can help authors reach a wider audience by creating more effective book covers and descriptions. AI-powered tools can analyze data on reader preferences and behaviors to create book covers that are more likely to catch the eye of potential readers. They can also analyze data on reader search queries and book descriptions to help authors create more effective book descriptions that better align with reader interests and preferences.

Overall, AI has the potential to be a powerful tool for authors looking to reach a wider audience and increase book sales. By utilizing AI-powered tools for social media management, email marketing, book advertising, and more, authors can create more effective marketing campaigns that are tailored to the needs and preferences of their target audience.

Sample book marketing plan with AI embedded:

1. Define your target audience: Use AI-powered data analysis tools such as Bookstat, PublishDrive, and Amazon KDP reports to analyze sales data and reader behavior. This can help you identify your target audience based on demographics, reading habits, and other factors.

2. Develop your author brand: Use AI-powered tools such as Canva and Adobe Spark to create visually appealing graphics and social media posts that reflect your author brand. You can also use AI-powered writing tools such as ProWritingAid and Grammarly to improve the quality of your writing and ensure consistency across all your marketing materials.

3. Build your author website: Use AI-powered website builders such as Wix and Squarespace to create a professional-looking website that showcases your books and author brand. You can also use AI-powered chatbots such as Tars to provide customer support and interact with your audience.

4. Develop your social media strategy: Use AI-powered social media management tools such as Hootsuite and Buffer to schedule posts and analyze engagement metrics. You can also use AI-powered advertising tools such as Facebook Ads and Google Ads to target specific audiences and drive traffic to your website.

5. Implement email marketing: Use AI-powered email marketing tools such as Mailchimp and Constant Contact to create targeted email campaigns that promote your books and engage your audience. You can also use AI-powered chatbots such as Drift and Intercom to

automate customer support and sales conversations.

6. Leverage book promotion sites: Use AI-powered book promotion sites such as BookBub and Goodreads to reach a wider audience and increase book sales. These sites use algorithms to recommend books to readers based on their reading preferences, which can help you reach a highly targeted audience.

7. Monitor and analyze results: Use AI-powered analytics tools such as Google Analytics and Hotjar to monitor website traffic, user behavior, and engagement metrics. This can help you identify areas for improvement and optimize your marketing strategy over time.

By incorporating AI-powered tools and technologies into your book marketing plan, you can reach a wider audience, improve the quality of your marketing materials, and optimize your campaigns for maximum impact and results.

Best practices for using AI tools for book promotion

When it comes to book promotion, there are some best practices to keep in mind when using AI tools. Here are some tips:

1. Use AI tools to personalize your marketing efforts: AI-powered email marketing tools can help you personalize your messages to individual readers, increasing the chances of engagement and conversion.

2. Don't rely solely on AI-generated content: While AI tools can be helpful in generating content, it's important not to rely on them entirely. Make sure to add your own personal touch to any content generated by AI.

3. Use AI tools to analyze and optimize your marketing efforts: AI-powered analytics tools can help you track the effectiveness of your marketing campaigns and make data-driven decisions about how to optimize them.

4. Always keep your target audience in mind: AI tools can help you identify your target audience and tailor your marketing efforts to their specific interests and preferences.

5. Stay up to date on the latest AI-powered marketing trends: As AI technology continues to evolve, new tools and techniques for book promotion are emerging all the time. Stay informed about the latest developments in the field to stay ahead of the curve.

By keeping these best practices in mind, authors can use

AI tools to effectively promote their books and reach a wider audience.

CHAPTER 12
AI AND READER ENGAGEMENT

In today's publishing industry, authors face an incredibly competitive market. The internet has made it easier than ever before for anyone to publish their writing, and the sheer volume of content available to readers is staggering. This means it's not enough to simply write a good book and hope readers will find it – authors need to actively engage with their readers in order to build relationships and create a loyal fanbase.

One of the most important reasons for authors to engage with their readers is to gain a deeper understanding of the market. By engaging with readers, authors can learn more about what types of books are popular, what readers are looking for in a book, and how they can better serve their audience. This information can be invaluable when it comes to marketing and promoting a book, as well as when planning future projects.

Additionally, engaging with readers can help authors build relationships with their audience. When readers feel connected to an author, they are more likely to become loyal fans and to recommend the author's work to others. This can lead to increased book sales and a more sustainable career as an author.

However, engaging with readers can be a time-consuming and challenging task, especially for authors who are already busy with writing and other aspects of the publishing process. This is where AI can be particularly helpful. AI-powered tools can help authors engage with readers in a more efficient and effective way, allowing them to build relationships and gather valuable information about the market without taking time away from writing.

Overall, reader engagement is a crucial component of success in the publishing industry. By actively engaging with their audience and using AI tools to do so, authors can gain a deeper understanding of the market, build relationships with readers, and ultimately increase book sales and build a sustainable career as an author.

This chapter will explore the ways in which AI can be used to enhance reader engagement for authors. We will delve into the various AI-powered tools and techniques that authors can utilize to deepen the connection with their readers and increase the success of their books.

AI has revolutionized the way we engage with content, and authors can use this technology to create personalized experiences for their readers. From chatbots to virtual book clubs, AI-powered tools can provide readers with new and unique ways to engage with books and authors.

This chapter will examine the role of AI in reader engagement, including how it can be used to enhance the reading experience, create meaningful connections between authors and readers, and even predict what readers want before they know it themselves.

We will discuss best practices for authors looking to incorporate AI into their reader engagement strategies. By the end of this chapter, readers will have a comprehensive understanding of the ways in which AI can be used to engage with readers and build a successful author platform.

Overview of AI-powered tools for reader engagement such as chatbots and personalized recommendations

AI-powered tools have made it easier than ever for authors to engage with their readers in meaningful ways. One of the ways in which AI can help with reader engagement is through the use of chatbots. These chatbots can be programmed to respond to a variety of queries from readers, including questions about the author's books and characters. They can also be used to provide recommendations based on the reader's preferences and reading history.

Another tool for reader engagement is personalized recommendations. AI algorithms can analyze a reader's reading habits and provide recommendations for books they may be interested in. This not only helps readers discover new books but also helps authors reach new readers who may be interested in their work.

AI-powered tools can also help authors engage with their readers through social media. These tools can analyze social media data to identify trends and topics of interest to readers, helping authors create content that resonates with their audience. They can also be used to automate social media posts, making it easier for authors to maintain an active social media presence.

Overall, AI-powered tools for reader engagement can help authors build stronger relationships with their readers, better understand the market, and ultimately sell more books.

Sample list of AI-powered tools for reader engagement and their descriptions:

1. IBM Watson: This tool uses natural language processing and machine learning to analyze text data from reader reviews and social media, providing sentiment analysis and insights for authors to improve their engagement strategies.
2. Parse.ly: This tool provides real-time analytics on reader behavior and engagement with online content, allowing authors to track the performance of their content and optimize their engagement strategies accordingly.
3. Sprout Social: This tool offers social media management and engagement features, including

automated messaging and personalized response recommendations based on user data.

4. Hootsuite Insights: This tool provides real-time social media monitoring and sentiment analysis, allowing authors to track how readers are responding to their content and adjust their engagement strategies accordingly.

5. Amazon Personalize: This tool uses machine learning algorithms to provide personalized book recommendations to readers based on their browsing and purchasing history on Amazon.

6. Zoho CRM: This tool offers customer relationship management features, including predictive analytics to help authors understand and anticipate their readers' preferences and behaviors.

7. Affinity: This tool uses machine learning to analyze reader behavior and preferences, providing personalized book recommendations and engagement strategies for authors to connect with their audience.

8. Persado: This tool uses natural language processing and machine learning to generate personalized messaging and content that resonates with individual readers.

9. Sailthru: This tool offers personalized marketing and engagement features, including predictive analytics to help authors understand

and anticipate their readers' needs and preferences.

10. RapidMiner: This tool provides data analytics and predictive modeling capabilities, allowing authors to analyze reader data and identify trends that can inform their engagement strategies.

These tools can help authors engage with readers in personalized, targeted ways, building a loyal fanbase and improving the overall success of their writing career.

How AI can help authors engage with readers and build their fanbase

AI can play a significant role in helping authors engage with readers and build a strong fanbase. Here are some ways in which AI-powered tools can help:

1. Personalized recommendations: AI-powered recommendation engines can analyze reader data to make personalized book recommendations based on the reader's reading habits and preferences. This can increase reader engagement and loyalty by providing them with books they are more likely to enjoy.

2. Chatbots: AI-powered chatbots can be used to provide quick and personalized responses to

readers' queries and concerns. Chatbots can also be used to send personalized book recommendations and reminders to readers. They can even be used to respond from a character in one of your books!

3. Social media management: AI-powered social media management tools can help authors analyze their social media engagement and performance. These tools can identify trends and patterns in engagement, suggest content to post, and help authors target specific reader demographics.

4. Sentiment analysis: AI-powered sentiment analysis tools can help authors understand their readers' reactions to their books and marketing campaigns. This can help authors tailor their messaging and marketing strategies to better resonate with their audience.

5. Predictive analytics: AI-powered predictive analytics can help authors forecast future trends and behaviors of their readers. This can help authors make data-driven decisions about marketing, publishing, and even writing styles.

Overall, AI-powered tools can help authors better engage with their readers, build a strong fanbase, and make data-driven decisions about their writing and publishing strategies.

CHAPTER 13
LANGUAGE TRANSLATION

L anguage translation is a crucial aspect of the publishing industry, especially in today's globalized world where access to books and literature is no longer restricted to a particular geographic region or language. The ability to communicate effectively and reach out to audiences in different parts of the world can help authors to broaden their readership and increase their revenue potential. It's not only important for authors, but it's also important for the industry as a whole as it promotes cultural exchange and diversifies the literary landscape.

Language translation is essential in making literature more accessible to people who are not fluent in the language of the original text. It allows authors to expand their audience and reach out to new readers who may not have been able to read their work otherwise. This is particularly important for authors who write in languages that are not widely spoken or are limited to a particular region.

Moreover, translation can play a vital role in promoting cultural exchange and increasing understanding between different nations and cultures. It can help readers to gain a better appreciation of the nuances of a particular culture and can promote cross-cultural dialogue. Translation can also help to preserve cultural heritage and promote diversity in literature by making works from different languages and cultures more widely available.

In the publishing industry, translation is not just about the literary value of a text, but also has significant economic implications. With the rise of e-commerce and digital publishing, it's now easier than ever for authors to reach a global audience. This has led to an increase in the demand for translations and has created new opportunities for publishers, translators, and authors.

In short, language translation is important for authors because it expands their readership, promotes cultural exchange, and increases revenue potential. It's also important for the publishing industry as a whole as it promotes diversity in literature and creates new opportunities for growth.

Chapter 13 focuses on language translation and the role that AI can play in this process. As the global market for books continues to expand, it is becoming increasingly important for authors to be able to reach readers who speak different languages. AI-powered language translation tools can help authors overcome this challenge by providing accurate and efficient translations of their work.

In this chapter, we will explore the various AI-powered tools and techniques available for language translation, as well as the potential benefits and challenges of using these tools. We will also examine real-world examples of how AI has been used in the language translation process in the publishing industry.

Overview of AI-powered language translation tools such as DeepL and Google Translate

Language translation is a crucial component for authors who wish to reach a global audience. With the rise of technology and the increasing demand for content in various languages, language translation has become an essential aspect of the publishing industry. In today's world, authors need to ensure their content is accessible to readers worldwide. This is where AI-powered language translation tools come in.

AI-powered language translation tools have revolutionized the translation process by providing accurate and efficient translations in a fraction of the time it takes a human translator. These tools have become increasingly sophisticated, utilizing machine learning algorithms to improve translation quality and speed. Among the most popular AI-powered language translation tools are DeepL and Google Translate.

DeepL is an AI-powered language translation tool that is renowned for its accuracy and natural-sounding translations. DeepL is unique in that it uses deep neural networks to translate text, which allows it to produce more accurate translations compared to other tools. It is also one of the fastest translation tools available, making it a popular choice for authors who need translations done quickly.

Google Translate is perhaps the most widely used AI-powered language translation tool in the world. It is a free tool that can translate over 100 languages, making it a popular choice for authors who want to translate their content into multiple languages. While its translations are not always perfect, it is constantly improving through machine learning algorithms that learn from user input.

Other AI-powered language translation tools worth mentioning include SDL Trados, MateCat, and Memsource. SDL Trados is a popular tool among professional translators, with a user-friendly interface and a range of advanced features that cater to the needs of translation professionals. MateCat is another free translation tool that is popular among freelance translators and small businesses. Memsource is a cloud-based translation management system that offers advanced features like project management and translation memory.

These tools have greatly simplified the language translation process, making it faster and more efficient. Authors can now easily translate their content into multiple languages with the click of a button, allowing them to reach a wider audience and increase their global presence. However, it's important to note that while AI-powered language translation tools have come a long way in terms of accuracy, they still have limitations, particularly when it comes to translating idiomatic expressions or culturally specific phrases.

In summary, AI-powered language translation tools have become an essential part of the publishing industry, allowing authors to reach a global audience with ease. While there are many tools available, each with its unique features and benefits, it is important for authors to choose the one that best fits their needs and ensures that their content is accurately translated to reach a wider audience.

sample list of AI-powered language translators along with a brief comparison of their quality:

1. Google Translate: One of the most well-known and widely used language translation tools, Google Translate offers translations in over 100 languages. While the accuracy can vary, it has improved significantly over the years with the use of AI.

2. DeepL: DeepL is another popular language translation tool that uses deep neural networks to provide more accurate translations. It currently supports translations in over 20 languages and is known for its high-quality translations.

3. Microsoft Translator: Microsoft Translator is an AI-powered language translation tool that supports over 60 languages. It uses machine learning to provide more accurate translations, and can even translate entire documents.

4. SDL Trados: SDL Trados is a professional translation tool used by many businesses and organizations. It uses AI-powered technology to improve the accuracy of its translations, and also provides features like translation memory and terminology management.

5. Systran: Systran is a language translation tool that uses AI and machine learning to provide more accurate translations. It supports over 130 languages and can be used for both personal and business use.

When it comes to comparing the quality of these language translation tools, it can be difficult to determine which is the "best" as it often depends on the specific language being translated, the context of the text, and other factors. However, in general, tools like DeepL and SDL Trados are often considered to provide higher-quality translations compared to more basic tools like Google Translate. It's also worth noting that while AI-powered language translation tools have improved significantly in recent years, they are still not perfect and may sometimes produce inaccurate or awkward translations.

How AI can help authors translate their work into different languages

AI-powered translation tools can save authors time and money, while also improving the quality and accuracy of translations. Here are some ways AI can help authors with language translation:

1. Automatic translation: AI-powered translation tools such as Google Translate and DeepL can automatically translate text from one language to another. These tools use machine learning algorithms to analyze patterns in the text and learn how to translate it accurately. Authors can use these tools to quickly translate their work into multiple languages.

2. Machine-assisted translation: AI-powered translation tools can also assist authors in the translation process. For example, SDL Trados and MemoQ are popular tools that use machine learning to suggest translations based on previous translations and glossaries. This can help authors save time and ensure consistency in their translations.

3. Neural machine translation: Neural machine translation (NMT) is an advanced type of machine translation that uses deep learning algorithms to

produce more accurate translations. NMT models are trained on large amounts of data and can understand the context of a sentence, resulting in translations that are more natural-sounding. Google Translate and DeepL both use NMT to produce high-quality translations.

4. Post-editing: AI-powered translation tools can also assist authors with post-editing, which involves reviewing and editing machine-translated text to improve its quality. This can be done by human translators or by the authors themselves using tools such as XTM and Smartling. AI-powered post-editing tools can help authors identify errors and suggest corrections to improve the quality of their translations.

Overall, AI-powered language translation tools can help authors reach a global audience by translating their work into different languages quickly and accurately. By using these tools, authors can save time and money while also ensuring that their translations are of high quality.

Best practices for using AI-powered language translation tools

When using AI-powered language translation tools to translate your work, it is important to keep the following best practices in mind:

1. Use high-quality source material: The quality of the translation will depend largely on the quality of the source material. Make sure your original text is well-written and free of errors.

2. Understand the limitations of the tool: While AI-powered language translation tools have come a long way, they are still far from perfect. Understand the limitations of the tool you are using and be prepared to edit and refine the translated text.

3. Avoid complex language and idioms: AI-powered translation tools often struggle with complex language and idioms, so try to keep your writing simple and straightforward.

4. Check for accuracy and context: Even the best AI-powered translation tools can make mistakes, so it is important to carefully review and edit the translated text to ensure accuracy and context.

5. Consider hiring a professional translator: While AI-powered translation tools can be a great starting point, consider hiring a professional

translator to refine the translated text and ensure it is culturally appropriate for the target audience.

By following these best practices, you can use AI-powered language translation tools to effectively translate your work and reach a wider audience in different languages.

The potential impact of AI-powered language translation on the global publishing industry

AI-powered language translation has the potential to revolutionize the global publishing industry by allowing authors to reach a wider audience in different countries and regions of the world. With the help of AI-powered language translation tools, authors can easily translate their work into multiple languages, thereby increasing their reach and impact.

One potential impact of AI-powered language translation on the publishing industry is the democratization of literature. With the ability to easily translate books into different languages, books from different cultures and countries can reach a wider audience, breaking down language barriers and promoting diversity in literature.

Another potential impact is the reduction of costs associated with traditional translation methods. Human translation is a costly and time-consuming process, but with the use of AI-powered translation tools, the process can be automated, reducing the time and costs associated with translation.

Additionally, AI-powered translation tools can provide more accurate translations compared to traditional methods. AI-powered translation tools can use machine learning algorithms to improve translation accuracy over time, resulting in better translations for readers.

Overall, AI-powered language translation has the potential to revolutionize the publishing industry by providing a more cost-effective, accurate, and efficient way to translate literature into different languages, ultimately promoting diversity in literature and enabling authors to reach a wider global audience.

PART IV
AFTERWORD

How AI can help authors in both writing and publishing

AI has revolutionized the publishing industry and has the potential to completely transform the way authors write and publish their work. By utilizing AI-powered tools, authors can improve their writing, collaborate more efficiently, analyze data insights, reach wider audiences, and engage with readers in a more meaningful way. However, as with any new technology, there are concerns about the role of AI in creative fields like writing, with some fearing that AI will replace human creativity and jobs.

Despite these concerns, the integration of AI in the writing process has already shown to be a game-changer for authors. For example, AI-powered brainstorming tools like GPT-3 and Jarvis can help authors generate ideas, create outlines, and provide content suggestions. These tools allow authors to expand their creativity and think outside the box, resulting in more unique and engaging content. Additionally, AI-powered collaboration tools like Google Docs and Slack can help authors work more efficiently with their editors, beta readers, and cover designers.

One of the most significant benefits of AI-powered tools for authors is the ability to analyze data insights. Tools like Bookstat, PublishDrive, and Amazon KDP reports can help authors track and analyze book sales, reader behavior, and market trends, allowing them to make informed decisions about their marketing strategies and future projects. This data can also help authors identify gaps in the market, better understand their target audience, and create content that resonates with readers.

AI-powered language translation tools like DeepL and Google Translate are also changing the game for authors, allowing them to translate their work into different languages with ease. This can help authors reach wider audiences and increase their book sales globally.

Despite the many benefits of AI, there are concerns that it could replace human creativity in the publishing industry. However, it is important to remember that AI is only a tool and cannot replace human creativity, voice, and perspective. Instead, AI can help enhance and expand human creativity, allowing authors to explore new ideas and reach new heights in their writing.

In order to make the most of AI-powered tools, authors should follow best practices for using them. This includes understanding the limitations of AI and using it as a tool to complement human creativity, rather than relying solely on it. Authors should also ensure that they are using high-quality AI-powered tools and staying up-to-date with new advancements in the field.

The potential impact of AI on the publishing industry and the future of publishing

AI has already transformed the publishing industry in many ways, and its potential impact continues to grow. With AI-powered tools, authors can enhance their writing process, from generating ideas to editing and proofreading. AI can also help authors discover new books, analyze the market, and reach a wider audience through book promotion and marketing. Additionally, AI-powered language translation can enable authors to translate their work into different languages and expand their readership globally.

However, some people are concerned that AI might replace human creativity and diminish the value of human effort in the publishing industry. They worry that AI-generated content might lack originality and authenticity, and that using AI could result in a homogenization of literature.

Despite these concerns, the benefits of AI-powered tools for authors and publishers are vast. AI can help authors overcome writer's block, generate fresh ideas, and improve the quality of their writing. AI can also provide publishers with valuable insights into the market and reader behavior, helping them to make informed decisions and optimize their business strategies.

In addition to improving the efficiency and effectiveness of the publishing industry, AI has the potential to open up new opportunities for innovation and creativity. By working in collaboration with AI, authors and publishers can enhance their creative processes and achieve greater success in a rapidly evolving industry.

The future of publishing is likely to be shaped by the continued development and implementation of AI-powered tools and technologies. As technology advances, we can expect to see even more sophisticated tools and applications that support and enhance the creative process of authors and publishers alike. However, it is important to remember that AI is a tool, not a replacement for human creativity and ingenuity. The successful integration of AI into the publishing industry will require a balance between technology and human insight, as well as ongoing discussion and ethical considerations to ensure that AI is used in a responsible and beneficial way.

The future of publishing is rapidly evolving as new technologies, including AI, are introduced to the industry. With the help of AI, the publishing industry is becoming more efficient, more personalized, and more accessible to readers across the globe. As AI technologies continue to advance, they will undoubtedly change the way books are written, edited, marketed, and distributed.

One potential future of publishing with AI is the development of highly personalized books. AI algorithms can be used to analyze reader data and generate highly personalized recommendations and reading lists. This could lead to a shift away from mass-market publishing towards more niche publications that cater to highly specific audiences.

Another potential future of publishing with AI is the development of highly automated production processes. AI tools can be used to streamline the writing, editing, and design processes, making the production of books faster and more efficient. This could lead to more books being produced, more quickly, and at lower costs, making it easier for authors to get their work published.

However, with all the benefits of AI in the publishing industry, there are also concerns. One of the biggest concerns is the potential loss of jobs in the publishing industry as more and more processes become automated. There are also concerns about the accuracy and reliability of AI-generated content, as well as the ethical implications of using AI to create highly personalized content.

Despite these concerns, the potential benefits of AI in the publishing industry are significant. As AI technologies continue to advance, we can expect to see new and innovative uses of these tools in the creation, production, and distribution of books. While the future of publishing with

AI is uncertain, one thing is clear: the publishing industry is set to undergo a significant transformation in the years to come, and AI will undoubtedly play a key role in shaping that future.

What's coming next

Personalization: AI-powered personalization will continue to be a key trend in marketing, allowing businesses to tailor their messaging and experiences to individual customers based on their behavior, preferences, and interests.

Voice search optimization: With the increasing popularity of smart speakers and voice assistants, AI-powered voice search optimization will become even more important for businesses looking to improve their online visibility and reach.

Chatbots and conversational AI: Chatbots and conversational AI will continue to gain traction as businesses look for ways to automate customer service and improve customer experiences.

Predictive analytics: AI-powered predictive analytics will help businesses to better understand their customers' behavior and preferences, allowing them to make more informed decisions about their marketing strategies.

Augmented Reality and Virtual Reality: AI-powered AR and VR technology will continue to evolve, creating more immersive and interactive experiences for customers, and providing businesses with new ways to engage with their audiences.

Call to action for authors to explore and experiment with AI in their writing and publishing careers.

As AI continues to revolutionize the publishing industry, it is important for authors to stay up-to-date on the latest advancements and opportunities available to them. By incorporating AI-powered tools and techniques into their writing and publishing process, authors can streamline their work, gain valuable insights, and ultimately reach a wider audience.

If you are an author looking to take advantage of the benefits of AI in your work, now is the time to explore and experiment with the tools and resources available. Start by researching the various AI-powered tools and software options that are tailored to your specific needs, whether it be for brainstorming, editing, book promotion, or translation.

Be sure to also keep an open mind about the potential impact that AI may have on the publishing industry as a whole, and consider how you can adapt and evolve your own strategies to stay ahead of the curve.

Finally, don't forget the importance of balancing AI with your own unique human creativity and perspective. While AI tools can certainly aid in the writing and publishing process, it is ultimately the author's creativity and individuality that sets their work apart and captures the attention of readers.

By incorporating AI into your writing and publishing process in a thoughtful and intentional way, you can position yourself for success in the ever-evolving publishing industry. So, take the plunge and embrace the exciting possibilities that AI has to offer for authors today!

CHAPTER 14
CASE STUDIES

Overcoming Writer's Block with AI-Powered Prompts: A Case Study of Mike's Creative Breakthrough

Introduction: Mike is an experienced author who has been working on a novel for several years. However, he has been struggling with writer's block and has been unable to make progress on his project. Despite his best efforts, he has been stuck on the same idea for a long time and can't seem to find a way to move forward. In this case study, we explore how Mike overcame his writer's block with the help of AI-powered prompts.

Challenge: Mike had been grappling with writer's block for years and was feeling increasingly frustrated and discouraged. He had tried various strategies to break free from his creative rut, including meditation, exercise, and brainstorming sessions with fellow writers. However, none of these techniques seemed to work, and Mike felt like he was running out of options.

Solution: Mike decided to try a new approach and turned to AI-powered prompts to help him overcome his writer's block. He used a tool that leverages GPT-4 technology to generate creative prompts that would inspire him to write new ideas. These prompts were tailored to Mike's interests and writing style, and provided a fresh perspective that helped him break out of his creative rut.

Tools Embraced:

1. GPT-4-powered writing prompts: Mike used OpenAI's GPT-4 language model, which analyzed his writing style and interests to provide tailored prompts for his work.
2. Articoolo: This AI-powered content creation tool analyzed existing content and generated suggestions for new and unique ideas.
3. Grammarly: Mike used this AI-powered tool to correct grammar, spelling, and punctuation errors, and receive suggestions for revisions.
4. Boomerang or Clara: These virtual writing assistants helped Mike handle administrative tasks such as scheduling, reminders, and research, freeing up his time for creative work.

By using these AI-powered tools, including GPT-4-powered prompts and Articoolo for content creation, Mike was able to overcome his writer's block and make significant progress on his novel. Grammarly helped him improve the quality of his writing, and virtual writing assistants helped him manage his time more effectively. Overall, these tools provided him with new inspiration, improved the quality of his work, and allowed him to focus more on the creative aspects of his writing.

Results: After using AI-powered prompts for several weeks, Mike was able to make progress on his novel. He wrote several new chapters that expanded on his original idea and introduced new characters and plot twists. He felt a renewed sense of motivation and purpose, and was excited to continue working on his project. Mike credits the use of AI-powered prompts for helping him overcome his writer's block and rediscover his passion for writing.

Conclusion: This case study highlights the potential of AI-powered prompts in overcoming writer's block and unlocking creative potential. For authors who have been struggling to make progress on their projects, AI can be a valuable tool for generating new ideas and breaking out of creative ruts. By leveraging the power of AI, authors can tap into a wealth of creative inspiration and achieve their writing goals.

Enhancing Creativity and Productivity with AI-Powered Writing Tools: A Case Study of Diane's Writing Journey

Introduction: Diane is a published author who has been writing for several years. However, she has been facing several challenges in her writing, including difficulty making word count, expanding on ideas, and developing complex storylines. Despite her experience and dedication, Diane felt like she had hit a creative wall and wasn't sure how to move forward. In this case study, we explore how Diane used AI-powered writing tools to overcome these challenges and enhance her creativity and productivity.

Challenge: Diane had been struggling with several writing challenges, including low word count, lack of inspiration, and difficulty developing complex storylines. She felt like her writing had become stagnant and predictable, and wasn't sure how to inject new life into her projects. She had tried various techniques, including writing exercises and research, but none seemed to work. Diane was determined to find a new approach to take her writing to the next level.

Solution: Diane decided to try AI-powered writing tools to help her overcome her writing challenges. She used a tool that leverages GPT-3 technology to generate writing prompts, suggest new storylines, and even write passages of text. These tools provided Diane with a fresh perspective on her writing, allowing her to develop new ideas, expand on her existing ones, and create complex storylines that she had never thought of before.

Tools Embraced:

1. OpenAI's GPT-4 language model: Diane used this tool to generate creative prompts, writing content, and edited written material. It helped her to overcome writer's block, generated unique and creative ideas, and provided suggestions for improving her writing.
2. Articoolo: Diane used this AI-powered content creation tool to expand her ideas and develop complex storylines. It provided her with suggestions for plot twists, character development, and other elements of her writing.
3. Boomerang: Diane used this virtual writing assistant to handle administrative tasks such as scheduling, reminders, and research, which helped her to free up her time for creative work.
4. Hootsuite: Diane used this social media management tool to schedule social media posts, analyze engagement metrics, and track social media performance. It helped her to promote her work, build her brand, and connect with her audience.

By using these specific AI-powered tools, Diane was able to enhance her creative process and take her writing to the next level. OpenAI's GPT-4 language model provided her with new ideas and plot twists, Articoolo helped her to develop her storylines, Boomerang allowed her to manage her time more effectively, and Hootsuite helped her to connect with her audience and promote her work effectively.

Results: After using AI-powered writing tools for several weeks, Diane was able to significantly improve her writing. She was able to meet her word count targets, develop new and complex storylines, and expand on her ideas in ways that she had never thought possible. Diane felt a renewed sense of inspiration and motivation, and was excited to continue working on her projects. She credits the use of AI-powered writing tools for helping her overcome her writing challenges and achieve her writing goals.

Conclusion: This case study demonstrates the potential of AI-powered writing tools in enhancing creativity and productivity for authors. For writers like Diane who have been struggling with writing challenges, AI can be a valuable tool for generating new ideas, expanding on existing ones, and creating complex storylines. By leveraging the power of AI, authors can tap into a wealth of creative inspiration and take their writing to new heights.

Combining Artistic Creativity with AI-Powered Tools: A Case Study of Isabelle's Journey to Embracing Technology

Introduction: Isabelle is a hardcore creative artist who is passionate about her work as an author, designer, and illustrator. She values the human touch and is wary of using technology in her creative process. However, she understands the potential of AI-powered tools to enhance her productivity and creativity, and is interested in finding a way to integrate them into her business. In this case study, we explore how Isabelle found a way to combine her artistic creativity with AI-powered tools to achieve her creative goals.

Challenge: Isabelle had been hesitant to use AI-powered tools in her creative work, as she felt that they might detract from the human element of her art. However, she also recognized the potential of these tools to help her work more efficiently and effectively. She was unsure of how to strike a balance between her love of traditional artistic methods and her desire to leverage technology to improve her work.

Solution: Isabelle decided to approach AI-powered tools with an open mind and an experimental mindset. She began using a tool that leverages GPT-4 technology to generate creative prompts for her writing, as well as image recognition and editing tools for her design and illustration work. She found that these tools provided her with a fresh perspective on her creative projects, allowing her to explore new ideas and techniques that she might not have thought of otherwise.

1. Canva: This AI-powered design tool allowed Isabelle to create professional-looking graphics,

posters, flyers, and other visual content quickly and easily. With its wide range of customizable templates, images, fonts, and icons, she was able to create visually appealing designs that helped her to convey her message effectively.

2. Copy.ai: This AI-powered content creation tool generated unique content based on Isabelle's input. Whenever she needed inspiration for a new blog post, social media update, or marketing copy, she turned to Copy.ai for fresh ideas. The AI-powered content creation tool generated optimized content that was both engaging and relevant, allowing her to focus on her creative work without spending hours on research and writing.

3. Boomerang: This virtual writing assistant handled administrative tasks such as scheduling, reminders, and research. With Boomerang's automated responses and integrated email and calendar features, Isabelle was able to manage her time more effectively and stay on top of important deadlines.

4. DeepArt.io: This AI-powered tool allowed Isabelle to transform her photos into works of art. It used a neural network to analyze the input image and apply a style transfer algorithm to make the photo look like it was painted in a specific style or by a specific artist. The benefit of

DeepArt.io was that Isabelle could create unique and visually stunning art pieces from her photos, which could be used in her design or illustration work.

By using these specific AI-powered tools, Isabelle was able to enhance her creative process and achieve better results. Canva allowed her to quickly create visually appealing designs, Copy.ai helped her to generate new ideas and content for her writing and design work, Boomerang helped her to manage her time more effectively, and Deep-Art.io allowed her to create unique and visually stunning art pieces from her photos. Overall, these tools provided her with the support she needed to enhance her creative process and take her artistic endeavors to the next level.

Results: After using AI-powered tools for several weeks, Isabelle was able to significantly improve her productivity and creativity. She found that the tools allowed her to work more efficiently and effectively, freeing up more time for her to focus on the aspects of her work that she enjoyed most. She also found that the tools allowed her to explore new artistic techniques and styles, expanding her creative repertoire in ways that she never thought possible. Elle now feels more comfortable using AI-powered tools in her creative work and is excited to continue experimenting with them in the future.

Conclusion: This case study highlights the potential of AI-powered tools to enhance artistic creativity and productivity, even for hardcore traditionalists like Isabelle . By approaching AI-powered tools with an open mind and an experimental mindset, artists like Isabelle can find a way to integrate technology into their creative process while still maintaining the human element that makes their art unique. The key is to find a balance between tradition and innovation, leveraging the power of AI to enhance creativity and achieve creative goals.

Embracing AI-Powered Tools to Enhance Author Support: A Case Study of Sam's Journey to Overcoming Technological Hesitation

Introduction: Sam is a personal assistant to several authors, and while she values the power of technology in her work, she has been hesitant to embrace AI-powered tools. However, she recognizes the potential of these tools to enhance her ability to support her clients and is interested in learning more about them. In this case study, we explore how Sam overcame her technological hesitation and embraced AI-powered tools to improve her work and support her clients.

Challenge: Sam had been hesitant to embrace AI-powered tools, feeling that they might be impersonal and take away from the human element of her work. However, she also recognized that AI-powered tools could help her work more efficiently and effectively, allowing her to provide better support to her clients. She was unsure of how to strike a balance between her traditional approach to her work and the potential benefits of these tools.

Solution: Sam decided to approach AI-powered tools with an open mind and a willingness to learn. She began researching different AI-powered tools that could help her work more efficiently and effectively, and started experimenting with them. She found that these tools provided her with new ways to manage her time, communicate with clients, and organize projects. Over time, she became more comfortable with these tools and started incorporating them into her work on a regular basis.

Tools Embraced:

1. Grammarly: An AI-powered tool that assists with grammar, spelling, and punctuation errors.
2. Trello: A project management tool that uses AI to help with task prioritization and organization.
3. Crystal Knows: A tool that uses AI to analyze personality traits and communication styles to help with client communication.
4. GPT-3-powered writing tools: These tools help with generating creative prompts, writing content, and editing written material.
5. Social media management tools: AI-powered tools that help with scheduling social media posts, analyzing engagement metrics, and tracking social media performance.

Results: After embracing AI-powered tools, Sam was able to significantly improve her efficiency and productivity. She was able to manage multiple projects simultaneously, communicate more effectively with clients, and generate creative ideas with greater ease. Her clients also noticed a difference in the quality of her work and appreciated the increased efficiency and responsiveness she was able to provide.

Conclusion: This case study demonstrates the potential of AI-powered tools in enhancing support for authors. By approaching these tools with an open mind and a willingness to learn, assistants like Sam can find ways to incorporate technology into their work while still maintaining the human element that makes their work unique. The key is to strike a balance between tradition and innovation, leveraging the power of AI to enhance productivity, communication, and creativity.

Revolutionizing Independent Publishing: Jacky's Journey with AI-Powered Tools.

Introduction: Jacky is the founder and CEO of a small publishing business that helps independent authors edit, develop, and market their books. Jacky faced challenges in meeting the increasing demand for the company's services while providing personalized attention to each author. To overcome these challenges, Jo decided to incorporate AI-powered tools into the company's operations.

Challenge: The publishing business faced several challenges that made it difficult to provide high-quality, personalized services to each author. Firstly, the company was experiencing rapid growth and increasing demand for its services. This led to a heavy workload for the editors, making it challenging for them to provide detailed feedback and personalized attention to each author. Secondly, the publishing landscape was rapidly changing, and the company needed to keep up with the latest trends in editing, development, and marketing to remain competitive. Finally, the company needed to find a way to improve the quality and efficiency of its services without sacrificing its commitment to personalized attention for each author.

Solution: Jacky decided to incorporate AI-powered tools into the company's operations to help improve the quality and efficiency of its services. By leveraging AI, the company could streamline its operations, provide better services to its clients, and achieve better results. The AI-powered tools allowed the editors to focus on more complex editing tasks, provide personalized feedback to the authors, and improve the overall quality of the manuscripts. By incorporating social media management tools, the company could promote the books more effectively and connect with the target audience more efficiently, resulting in increased book sales and better visibility for the authors. Finally, by using AI-powered design tools, the company could create visually appealing book covers and marketing materials that helped the books to stand out from the competition and attract more readers.

Tools embraced:

1. Grammarly: AI-powered editing tool to improve the quality and consistency of the authors' writing.
2. IBM Watson Natural Language Understanding: NLP tool to analyze the authors' manuscripts and provide feedback on the clarity and coherence of the writing.
3. Hootsuite: Social media management tool to improve the authors' book marketing efforts.
4. Canva: AI-powered design tool to create professional-looking book covers and marketing materials.

Results: By leveraging these AI-powered tools, Jo was able to provide better editing, development, and marketing services to the authors. The tools allowed the editors to focus on more complex editing tasks, provide personalized feedback to the authors, and improve the overall quality of the manuscripts. The social media management tool helped the company to promote the books more effectively and connect with the target audience more efficiently, resulting in increased book sales and better visibility for the authors. Finally, the AI-powered design tool allowed the company to create visually appealing book covers and marketing materials, helping the books to stand out from the competition and attract more readers.

Conclusion: Jacky's use of AI-powered tools helped to streamline the company's operations, provide better services to its clients, and achieve better results. The power of AI allowed the company to improve the quality and efficiency of its services, helping the authors to achieve their writing and publishing goals. By embracing AI, Jacky's company is better positioned to meet the challenges of a rapidly changing publishing landscape and to help independent authors succeed.

CHAPTER 15
RESOURCE GUIDE

Get the AI Tools you need

1. AI-powered writing and editing tools:

- Grammarly: A popular tool that uses AI to check for grammar and spelling errors.
- Hemingway: An app that analyzes your writing and provides suggestions for improving clarity and readability.
- ProWritingAid: A writing assistant that uses AI to help you improve your writing style and detect errors.
- Atomic AI: A tool that uses AI to analyze your writing and provide insights into how you can improve it.

- Copysmith: A tool that uses AI to generate marketing copy and product descriptions.

1. AI-powered book marketing and promotion tools:

- BookBub: A platform that uses AI to recommend books to readers based on their preferences.
- Reedsy Discovery: A tool that helps authors promote their books to a targeted audience using AI algorithms.
- PubMatch: A tool that connects authors with publishers and agents using AI-powered matching algorithms.
- Book Brush: A tool that uses AI to help authors create professional-looking graphics for book promotion.
- NetGalley: A platform that uses AI to help publishers and authors promote their books to a community of avid readers.

1. AI-powered translation and language tools:

- DeepL: A machine translation tool that uses neural networks to produce high-quality translations.
- Google Translate: A popular translation tool that uses AI to provide translations in multiple

languages.

- SDL Trados: A translation software that uses AI to help translators work more efficiently.
- MemoQ: A translation software that uses AI to help translators improve their productivity and accuracy.
- SYSTRAN: A tool that provides machine translation services for businesses and individuals using AI-powered algorithms.

1. AI-powered book discovery tools:

- Goodreads: A platform that uses AI algorithms to recommend books to readers based on their reading preferences.
- Book Riot: A book discovery site that uses AI to help readers find new books to read.
- Novel Effect: An app that uses AI to provide an immersive reading experience by adding sound effects and music to books.
- Amazon Kindle: An e-reader that uses AI to provide personalized book recommendations and to help authors promote their books.

Go Deep on AI Geekness

AI-related resources to enjoy on your AI journey:

1. AI subreddit: r/artificial is a popular subreddit dedicated to the discussion of artificial intelligence.
2. AI conferences: conferences like NeurIPS, ICML, and CVPR are top conferences in the field of AI, and can be a great way to stay up to date on the latest research and trends.
3. AI newsletters: newsletters like AI Weekly, Machine Learning Weekly, and Import AI are popular newsletters that provide updates on the latest developments in AI.
4. AI books: there are many great books on AI, including "The Master Algorithm" by Pedro Domingos, "Superintelligence" by Nick Bostrom, and "Machine Learning Yearning" by Andrew Ng.
5. AI podcasts: podcasts like "Data Skeptic", "Artificial Intelligence in Industry", and "This Week in Machine Learning and AI" are popular podcasts that discuss AI-related topics.
6. AI online courses: online courses like Coursera's "Machine Learning" and edX's "Artificial Intelligence" are popular courses that offer in-depth learning on AI and machine learning.
7. AI blogs: blogs like OpenAI, AI Trends, and MIT Technology Review are popular blogs that discuss AI and its impact on society.

8. AI research papers: arXiv is a popular repository of academic research papers in the field of AI, which can be useful for researchers or those looking to stay up to date on the latest research.

Prompts for GPT-4

There are several resources available for authors who want to learn more about prompts for GPT-4 or AI in general. Here are some options to consider:

- OpenAI's GPT-4 Demo: OpenAI offers a free GPT-4 demo on their website, which allows you to experiment with different prompts and see how GPT-4 generates responses. This can be a helpful way to get a feel for how the technology works.
- OpenAI's GPT-4 Playground: This is a web-based environment that allows users to experiment with GPT-4 by inputting different prompts and seeing the output. The Playground also provides helpful tips and examples for using GPT-4 effectively.
- AI Dungeon: This is a platform that uses GPT-4 to generate interactive stories based on user inputs. Users can input prompts and then watch as the AI generates a story based on those prompts.

- Hugging Face's Transformers Library: This is an open-source library that provides access to several different pre-trained AI models, including GPT-4. The library also provides helpful resources for getting started with AI and NLP.
- The AI Guild: This is a community of AI professionals and enthusiasts who share resources and information about all things AI. The Guild offers online courses, webinars, and other resources for learning about AI and using tools like GPT-4.
- OpenAI's GPT-4 API: This is a paid service that provides access to GPT-3's full capabilities. The API can be used to create custom AI-powered applications or to integrate GPT-4 into existing tools and platforms.

OVERALL, there are many resources available for learning about and using GPT-4 and other AI tools. By exploring these resources, bloggers and other content creators can stay up-to-date with the latest developments in AI and incorporate these tools into their work in new and exciting ways.

Unfortunately, as an AI language model, I do not have access to the specific source of this information. However, the mentioned resources can be easily found through a quick online search.

ABOUT AI4 AUTHORS

We are passionate about helping authors stay ahead of the curve when it comes to the latest technologies and advancements in the publishing industry. Our team is made up of experienced authors, marketers, publishers and technology experts who understand the unique challenges and opportunities that arise in today's fast-paced digital landscape.

We believe that embracing AI can help authors at every stage of the book creation process, from generating ideas and developing characters to marketing and distribution. By providing training and resources tailored specifically to the needs of authors, we aim to empower writers to take advantage of the latest tools and techniques to improve their craft and reach new audiences.

With a commitment to innovation, integrity, and a love for great storytelling, we are dedicated to helping authors navigate the exciting and ever-evolving world of publishing. Whether you are a seasoned writer or just starting out, our team is here to support you every step of the way as you harness the power of AI to create and share your stories with the world.

ABOUT THE AUTHOR

Author, Marketer, Publisher, Teacher

Jamie is a USA Today bestselling author with a passion for helping other authors succeed. She is the owner of Dragon Realm Press, a publishing house that specializes in working with indie authors. With over a decade of experience in the publishing industry, Jamie has become an expert in book marketing, book design, and book editing. Her approach is centered on creating a personalized and collaborative experience for her clients that results in high-quality, marketable books.

Her extensive marketing background allows her to guide authors through the complex world of book promotion, providing them with strategies that work. Jamie believes that every author has a unique voice, and she is committed to helping them share their stories with the world.

With a focus on innovation, Jamie has been at the forefront of integrating AI into the publishing industry. She believes that AI is a powerful tool that can help authors streamline their processes and reach new audiences. Jamie is passionate about helping authors navigate the ever-changing landscape of publishing and achieve their goals.

ABOUT THE AUTHOR

Author, Technologist, Marketer, Publisher

Melle has spent her career translating complex technology for the lay person, working with prestigious organizations such as NASA, Northrop Grumman, and Hewlett Packard. As the Marketing Director for an AI-enabled app company, Melle continues to leverage technology to drive meaningful change. She believes we are at a pivotal moment in history, where the incredible potential of AI is set to revolutionize the way we work and live. Melle is passionate about helping people navigate this shift and harness the power of AI to achieve their goals. Her expertise and unique perspective make her an invaluable resource for anyone looking to tap into the full potential of AI in their personal or professional life.

Outside of her professional career, Melle is a USA Today bestselling author, having published multiple books with rave reviews through a fresh approach to fantasy storytelling. Through her work as an author, Melle has gained a deep understanding of the writing and publishing process, and how emerging technologies like AI can support and enhance the creative process. She is excited to share her expertise and insights with fellow authors in the AI for Authors community.

www.ingramcontent.com/pod-product-compliance
Lightning Source LLC
LaVergne TN
LVHW051331050326
832903LV00031B/3477